HOW TO
NAVAL OFFICER

By
REAR ADMIRAL YATES STIRLING, Jr.
U.S.N., Retired

ROBERT M. McBRIDE & COMPANY
New York

Photographs by courtesy of:

THE UNITED STATES NAVY
THE UNITED STATES MARINE CORPS
THE UNITED STATES NAVAL ACADEMY
THE UNITED STATES COAST GUARD
WIDE WORLD PHOTOS

Midshipmen of the U. S. Naval Academy present arms during the ceremonies attending the annual presentation of colors.

CONTENTS

v

CONTENTS

HOW TO BE A NAVAL OFFICER

CHAPTER I

THE NAVY AS A PROFESSION

THE fleet's in—battleships, cruisers, destroyers in the harbor. And whether New York or New Orleans, San Francisco or San Diego, the scene is exciting to anyone who loves the sea. Ships that are a part of Uncle Sam's Navy are at anchor. Crowds gather to watch the sailors and officers at work on the decks. At dusk the signal lights in the rigging begin to wink, carrying on their mysterious conversation. Officers and men on shore leave take to the launches and are soon walking through the streets—back home after colorful months in the Philippines, China, Spain, South America, and other ports of call.

To every landlocked citizen, this is always a stirring picture—and at the same time, a comfortable picture, especially at this moment, with war in all the oceans of the world.

To you—to the young man who wants to be a naval officer—it has a special significance and excitement. You envy these officers you see returning from the ends of the earth. You know they have ridden rough seas, sliced through limitless fog, battled raging storms. You envy their knowledge of the mechanical mysteries of great guns, torpedoes, submarines, mines, navigation instruments. You know they have probably walked through the narrow streets of Havana or Santiago. Perhaps they've

9

ridden in a ricksha or in one of the wood-burning locomotives in Brazil. Perhaps they've danced on a moonlit
terrace in Rio de Janeiro. Perhaps they've had tea with
an ambassador or a charge d'affaires in Hongkong. All
these things in a naval officer's life are mixed together
in one vague, romantic jumble. You envy the officers' cos-
mopolitan calm, their fit look, their air of salty strength.
You sense the stout and honorable tradition they have
inherited from the great officers of our Navy, from Admiral George Dewey, Commodore John Paul Jones, and
the many others whose names form the Honor Roll of
American naval history. You know that the Navy, in war
and in peace, has always played a great and often glorious
part in the history of the United States. And you know
that today—with the tremendous importance being
placed on the defense of our shores—the Navy has need
of more and better men. You think you would like to
serve your country as a naval officer.

You have your goal, and you want to know how to
achieve it. To tell you is the function of this book.

Perhaps, knowing more of life in the army, which is
usually closer at hand and more easily observed, you
look upon the Navy as some peculiar organization that
is entered by a form of magic. You look at a naval officer
and you wonder how he became one. Was it an accident
of birth? Did his uncle attend the Naval Academy at
Annapolis? Or did his father know an influential Con-
gressman?

The truth is that he achieved his position by no such
easy means. His progress wasn't even mysterious. He
simply won his rank by systematic and hard application
to an ideal. He worked with tremendous energy. First

in entrance examinations, then at the Naval Academy and during service with the fleet, he demonstrated again and again that he had the stuff—and it's tough stuff—of which naval officers are made. So the insignia he wears is no accident, for nowhere are the basic principles of democracy more rigidly followed than in the military service of our country. All that this naval officer has done you can do, too, if—

At the beginning it's well to understand that you have set yourself an exacting course and to decide what you expect from life. If you would like wealth, if you would like to spend the rest of your life in one quiet spot, or if you prefer thought to action, you might as well forget about the Navy. Navy life will never give you a big bank account and it will never give you a chance to get your roots in the soil.

But it will give you a number of things the wealthiest man on earth cannot buy. As a naval officer you will be sure of a job so long as you do your job well and continuously qualify yourself for higher rank by diligent and faithful service. You can be dismissed neither by politics nor business conditions. World disarmament alone can affect you—and in these days of almost universal strife that is a remote possibility.

The sea, hard work, good food, and thorough physical training will equip you for the full enjoyment of life; your health will be ten times better than that of the average office worker. And if you are sick or injured, you will have no doctor's bills but will be well cared for in a modern naval hospital at the government's expense, and will continue to draw your salary. You will always be given a place to live, at no expense. On shipboard you will be assigned a cabin; on shore a sum of money will be added to your salary for rent. Uncle Sam will provide a comfortable pension for you when the time comes.

You will never be forced to stand still in the Navy, but will always be learning, acquiring further practical training, advancing in almost any skill or profession you could find in civilian life. For the Navy is a world in itself, a thousand cities afloat, with every branch of knowledge contributing to its efficient maintenance and effective operation.

These are the chief advantages of a naval career. There are others, harder to describe but no less important to you. No one can serve in the Navy without a deep sense of personal satisfaction—an added measure of strength that comes from the realization that you are doing a big job, performing a service that is honorable and important to the defense of our great country.

And, as you travel, you will appreciate the greatness of your country more and more. While associating with men of other nations, observing other races, and coming to a wider human understanding, you will see your country in a new perspective. You will develop an increasing respect for its virtues and advantages. You will realize that you are lucky to live in a country which guarantees every individual the right to life, liberty, and the pursuit of happiness—something that is becoming rarer and rarer over the earth's surface. After several years in foreign lands, you will understand the catch that comes in the throat of every man on shipboard, and the little tingle that races up his spine, when the boatswain's whistle pipes and the hoarse-throated boatswain's mates call, "All hands up anchor for home!"

The decision to become a naval officer takes careful thought and acute self-analysis; the life has romance, excitement, strong obligations to duty, and sacred traditions to uphold. The rewards are plentiful. But to be a naval officer you must be exceptional in many ways— more than you would have to be to succeed in most other professions. Physically and mentally you must be first-rate, and the careful program by which future officers are examined and trained quickly weeds out all who lack the proper qualifications. The men who command our Navy are exceptional men trained in much more than the mere mechanics of sailing a ship and firing a gun. In general education, moral and physical courage, in leadership and initiative, these men are far above the average. They have to be, for today more than ever before, our Navy is faced with an important job and a big one— the defense of the country at one of the most critical periods in the history of the world. But no possible invasion of the United States can very well succeed unless the Navy is completely destroyed or bottled up in a port by a superior force. And that isn't likely to happen as long as our naval officers are of such high calibre. There is room for many more like them at the top—and in any of the hundreds of departments upon which the strength of our sea power depends—for young men of spirit who have courage, aptitude, and are willing to school themselves well. You may have what it takes. Let's see.

CHAPTER II

PREPARATION AND CHARACTERIS-
TICS NECESSARY FOR A
NAVAL CAREER

IF YOUR heart is set on becoming a naval officer, the chances are that you already possess many of the personal qualifications desirable and necessary. You undoubtedly are determined, knowing that it is a difficult goal. You undoubtedly have a thirst for a life of excitement and peril—otherwise you would be looking toward a quieter, less dangerous career—perhaps farming or civil engineering or business. The hazardous nature of the calling appeals to you. You can feel the thrill of several hundred men racing to their stations as a crisp command crackles across the decks. You can hear the big guns booming out across the water.

This means you have one of the important basic qualities of a naval officer—a taste for adventure. You must realize, however, that that is scarcely enough, that other qualities must be awakened and developed.

You must realize that a naval officer, above all else, is a leader of men. This is his vital duty. He spends his entire career studying and performing that function. He must be the sort of leader described by Jomini, the great French historian and military leader: "A man of high moral courage capable of great resolutions. A physical courage which takes no account of danger. A man who is gallant, just, firm, upright, capable of esteeming merit in others without jealousy."

14

Warships and their officers see all kinds of scenery. Here the heavy cruiser USS *Augusta* is framed between two palm trees as it lies at anchor in Pearl Harbor in the Hawaiian Islands.

The USS *Quincy* is one of our most modern heavy cruisers, a fighting ship thoroughly streamlined to give it the maximum speed. Even the paint used internally, aluminum paint, was the lightest that could be employed. Launched in 1935, it weighs 9,375 tons, has an overall length of 588 feet, carries a complement of 551 officers and men, and travels at about 32 knots maximum.

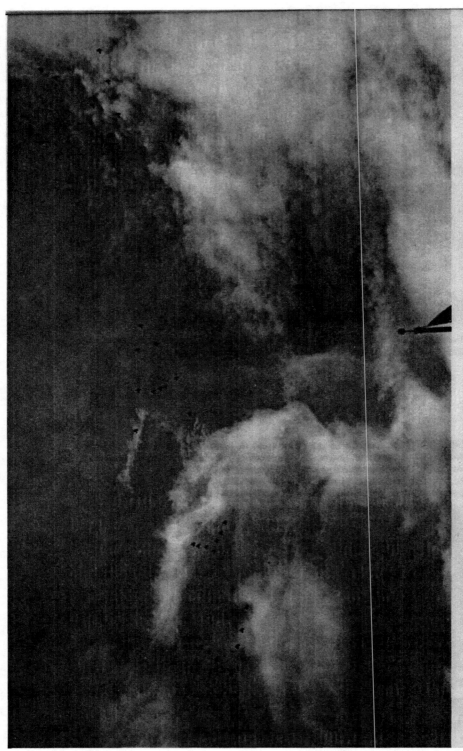

Army planes spelling out the word "Navy" in the sky when the author left his post at Pearl Harbor, Hawaii, in 1932.

The great military and naval leaders of history possessed such moral and physical power to a high degree. Of the two qualities, moral power is by far the more important; we call it *strength of character.*

Decision and good sense are important things for us to cultivate. They assure clearness in the conception of a task, and energy in its execution. After making a decision, a quality that contributes most to success is stubbornness. John Paul Jones, on board the sinking American warship *Bonhomme Richard,* and engaged in a death struggle with the British *Serapis* during the war with England, stubbornly answered when asked if he would surrender, "I have not yet begun to fight." Moral power won for him the victory.

General U. S. Grant, commanding the Union Armies in the Civil War, showed this important trait of character—stubbornness—when he announced: "We'll fight it out on this line if it takes all summer."

We must never forget that a leader can use his moral power correctly only when he is thoroughly versed in his profession, when he has acquired the needed confidence in his ability to succeed in any undertaking. Knowledge alone is not enough. One who would be a leader must frequently apply his knowledge to cases; in other words he must solve and execute problems dealing with the elements and principles of his profession. All great leaders have been students of history, adding historical problems to their personal experience.

In order to know the standard of character desired in officers of our Navy, let us read an often quoted paragraph of the Navy's Articles for the Government of the Navy:

"The Commanders of all fleets, squadrons, naval stations and vessels belonging to the Navy are required to show in themselves a good example of *virtue, honor, patriotism, and subordination.*"

These four cardinal qualities of character are important ingredients of leadership. No one can be truly great without all of them. Virtue denotes manliness, valor, courage, bravery. "Add to your faith, virtue, and to your virtue, knowledge," is a good recipe for *military character.* "The brave man is not he who feels no fear, but he whose noble mind its fear subdues," as one famous military leader of history once subdued his knees. Brave though he was, he had difficulty controlling his knees when going into battle. They trembled so violently he was often afraid his fellow-soldiers would notice and think he lacked courage. One day, before a battle, he was overheard saying to himself, "Tremble, legs, but if you only knew where I am about to take you, you would give way under me!"

With *virtue* as a foundation, *honor* erects a high sense of duty, a subconscious understanding of what is right and just, a sense of loyalty, fair dealing and faithfulness to trust. With *honor* an officer does not have to look for reward or punishment in the performance of a duty, but has only to execute the task scrupulously and for the task's sake.

There is one thing that must be innate in the soul of a naval officer. He should have obtained it in his mother's milk, yet it can be acquired through environment and instruction. That is *patriotism*—the motive binding us all together in one great cause. *Patriotism* among the armed forces of a nation gives unity to

Admiral Claude C. Bloch, Commander-in-Chief, U. S. Fleet and Captain
Robert A. Theobold, Chief of Staff, studying a fleet problem on the bridge
of the USS Pennsylvania, Flagship of the Fleet.

The study of various methods of communication is an essential part of the training of every "future Admiral." Ship-to-ship messages are often sent by means of a manually operated blinker.

The fleet of hydroplanes at Annapolis used in teaching the "middies" the art of flying.

action. This "feeling in the heart," bringing virtue to the civil administrators and self-sacrifice to the soldiers and sailors, is the bond of men who consider their nation as an entity. A truly patriotic citizen delights to identify himself with his nation's fortunes, to share in its triumphs and mourn in its disasters. He will ever look to the future when the nation's destiny will be fulfilled. This noble concept of "Country" represents a heritage of sentiments, of traditions, of thought, of common interest. Patriotism is fundamental. All of us must learn in our childhood to cherish and defend this most sacred of all national ideals.

A nation in whose citizens the virtue of patriotism is securely implanted will be strong, vigorous, progressive. Lacking this ideal, a nation will be weak and spineless— two traits of national character which inevitably lead to national death. Patriotism should be a passion which burns undiminished. True patriotism exerts so great an influence for unity that it is the moving force in war, an ideal for which soldiers and sailors, locked in battle with the foe, die cheerfully.

Patriotism has its distant roots in those times when a community existed only on the condition that one portion of the inhabitants stood guard while the remainder worked in the fields. There was always the risk that an attack from an enemy might come suddenly upon a weak spot in the defense and overwhelm it. To prevent annihilation of the tribe, therefore, the soldier guards were called upon to fight to the last man in order to give time for their comrades, scattered in the fields, to come to their support. It was in this manner that the idea of self-sacrifice for the good of the greater number first had

its origin, and it is the bed-rock foundation today of the
soldier's and sailor's calling.

Another indispensible quality is *subordination*. It is
the habit of obedience and is requisite among those in a
military service such as the Navy. It regulates the relations of subordinates to leaders; without it there can be
no discipline.

Many ignorant persons will endeavor to class subordination with slavery. Edmund Burke, the great Parlia-
mentarian, has glorified this attribute of good citizen-
ship in words so stirring as to confound the libertine and
appeal to every patriot. He calls the quality of subordination, "that generous loyalty to rank and sex, that
proud submission, that dignified obedience, that subordination of the heart, which has kept alive, even in servi-
tude itself, the spirit of exalted freedom."

In order to be able to lead, strong *will* is an essential;
power over others is founded upon will. The person who
leads is the person who knows best how to give the
most definite expression to his will. A demand upon
others, made with determination, seldom meets with op-
position. It has something impressive in it for those
who are to obey, something from which they attain
a sense of personal security that enhances their courage
and capacity.

Strong will must be coupled with self-confidence. We
must always have the courage of our convictions. Once
our mind is made up, there must be no faltering in the
execution. The self-confident mind is clouded with no
doubts or fears of the result; it acts with promptitude
and decision.

Ambition has been called the soldier's virtue. It is a

desire to excel, to be the first. Great deeds are impossible without ambition.

Other contributions to leadership are *patience* and *resolution* which are needed to "meet with triumph and disaster and treat those two imposters just the same."

And *imagination* will put the crowning glory upon the head of a leader of men. It is the creative force.

Here we have outlined the qualities that go to make up a military character. If you want to become a naval officer you may well hesitate when you learn what a perfect individual you must be if you are to become a leader of men. But remember that military character is a product developed by gradual and prolonged application, and what others have achieved you too can cultivate. The qualities needed in a leader do not shine forth except after profound study, and in the beginning, like every creature that tries to walk, the novice in the naval art is obliged to follow a guide. Of course there does exist the true genius, who differs from the common man in that he may sooner dispense with his guide, to become in his own turn the creator. Yet even a genius never ceases to develop his mind.

In order that a fleet of warships of many types may be led into battle as a unified force and the fleet's efforts at many points be directed by many individuals, what qualities of character are required in the leaders?

First and foremost, there must be the free acceptance of the plan, which means loyalty to the supreme leader. Thus having gained unity in thought, the effort must be continued until the end has been reached. To accomplish this, *decision of character* is demanded. An action once begun must not be abandoned. A pause or a change of plan, through indecision, robs the blow of the greater part of its force.

Military and naval operations, though, require more than mere loyalty. In a large force of battleships, aircraft carriers, cruisers, destroyers, and submarines, going into action against an enemy's fleet, there is no time for the supreme naval leader to attend to every detail of the impending battle. Subordinate leaders must appreciate the situation and act appropriately for themselves. It must be evident therefore that in the naval battle the forces of mentality and character enter most frequently, and are the dominating forces for success. The enemy must be opposed at every point. Subordinate leaders must act upon their own initiative. Not independently, but in coördinate effort. This quality so necessary in naval leadership is called *"trained initiative."* It is based upon full knowledge of the naval profession and complete loyalty to the plan of the supreme leader. It implies loyalty to a mission; an end in view—victory.

We have often heard it said of men in high positions: "He lacks decision of character." We have all known men who could not give a decided answer to the least important question, where action was concerned. Instead they would hide behind such answers as, "I'll think it over," or "I'll take the matter under consideration." Such men destroy unity in a naval organization. They undermine confidence and fritter away valuable time. They dissipate their own energy and the energy of their subordinates through "resolutions adopted, rejected, resumed, suspended."

Decision of character is the habit of dealing with each situation as it arises with a prompt, clear, and firm reply as to what shall be done and the manner of doing it. It is a habit which requires cultivation by practice. In the cultivation of this valuable habit—a most important one for any man who is in a position of responsibility, no matter how unimportant the position may be—the first thing to consider is: "What is the task?" Then: "What are the obstacles in the way of its accomplishment?" Further, a knowledge of, and a careful weighing of, the means at hand for overcoming the obstacles are required. Then we are ready by a simple process of reasoning to give a reply.

The novice in the Navy may find the process of reasoning long and laborious, for he has not acquired the knowledge of the obstacles or the means at hand of overcoming them. Knowledge and practice will overcome these difficulties. A trained mind can estimate a situation almost spontaneously. His decision or reply to a question will come so quickly after the question is put to him that it will appear to have been rendered almost without reasoning. Such is not the case; the trained mind "short circuits" from the recognition of the task to the reply. The reasoning is accomplished subconsciously, almost with the speed of light itself.

We have given *initiative* as one of the prime necessities for a naval officer. Initiative is of two kinds: (1) the power to make starts; and (2) the power to act upon one's own responsibility in order to help a bigger cause than one's own personal one. The second of these is called "trained initiative," and is arrived at through systematic study, through education to be exact, in order to have a grasp of the principles underlying the naval profession, only upon which this initiative can be built.

Without a clear understanding of these principles, initiative must inevitably lead to a disorganizing independence. We know that a child must not be given complete initiative in his attitude toward life. In his mind the moral and material principles of life have not yet been fully learned. Our aim, then, should be to confine his experiments in initiative to reasonably shallow water, and near enough home. It would be a most salutary experience for him to accept his own risks and to get figuratively speaking capsized, provided he did not thereby lose his young life. Thus he will learn the wind's treachery, the water's danger and discomfort, and his own poor judgment and insufficiency, without too seriously jeopardizing the lives of others or losing confidence in himself. A boy needs to buy as cheaply as possible the necessary experience of failure—thus tempering his wilfulness, developing his caution, cultivating his dexterity in handling his own craft (himself), and sharpening his judgment and his quickness of decision. In this way he will gain a working knowledge of the difficult world.

For the naval profession, initiative must be acquired in time of peace through frequent practice. It is a very old saying that "we learn from our failures, not from our successes." No one should be ashamed of a failure that occurred through a lack of knowledge, not through one's own negligence. Also, you should not depend upon learning the many lessons of life through the failures of yourself alone. You can profit by the failures of others.

One is never too young to begin character training. The Navy sets a high mark for you. Begin now to train yourself in the mental characteristics demanded by the naval service of its naval officers.

In preparing oneself for a career as a naval officer, the lives of our naval men of prominence in both peace and war should be studied. Such men as John Paul Jones, Isaac Hull, William Brainbridge, David Porter, John Rodgers and Stephen Decatur, fighting our naval ships for the "freedom of the sea" and "sailor's rights" on the sea; Perry, on Lake Erie, fighting the enemy, with James Lawrence's last words, "Don't give up the ship," written on the flag at the masthead of his flagship. There are many other naval heroes. Some have been immortalized in books, but many are unsung except in gallant words handed down in Naval traditions.

The war records of our Navy can be found in many volumes in libraries throughout the country. You should know of Farragut in the Civil War, Sampson, Schley and Dewey in the war with Spain, and Sims during the World War.

In all of these men, military character was developed to a high degree. A study of their lives will show you what qualities our Navy is looking for in its future officers and—if you are sincere—cement your determination to go forward.

CHAPTER III

THE WAY TO OBTAIN AN APPOINT-
MENT TO THE NAVAL ACADEMY

ONCE you have made up your mind that above all else you want a commission in the United States Navy, and once you have decided that you possess the necessary qualities, your course lies dead ahead and the going is rough. The first thing to do is to obtain an appointment to the United States Naval Academy at Annapolis, Maryland.

If that appointment were easy to obtain, the standards of our Navy would not be so high. But it is a difficult goal. For one thing, you will be in competition with thousands of other young men who have the same idea every year. And the requirements are exacting. The original appointment, however, and the commission that lies ahead, are both goals worth fighting for. To reach them, like every other worthwhile objective in life, will take what may seem like superhuman effort, but if you have the qualities demanded of a naval officer they will help you over all the hurdles. Don't give up until you have achieved success or found it impossible to attain. And don't depend entirely on your parents or others to help you in the first great step—the appointment to the Naval Academy. If you really want it, you will have to exert yourself first. You will need personality, earnestness, and perseverance.

The United States Naval Academy is maintained by

The United States Naval Academy at Annapolis, Maryland, from the air. Located on the Severn River, with a good anchorage for everything from sailboats to battleships, it is admirably situated to serve its purpose: the schooling of our future captains and admirals. In the foreground is Bancroft Hall, housing both classrooms and dormitories, one of the most beautiful and efficient government buildings in the country. Beyond it is the Administration Building, to the right the gymnasium, power plants, and the boat-basin. Seaplanes used for training may be seen on the Severn in the background.

A close-up of Bancroft Hall.

Midshipmen marching to afternoon recitations in the Administration Building.

Midshipmen in mess formation, ready to march to the Mess Hall.

The midshipman's alarm clock—the Academy Drum and Bugle Corps which sounds reveille, tattoo, and all the various calls between.

The memorial window to Admiral Farragut in the Chapel, one of the many memorials honoring naval heroes of the past which are the midshipman's constant inspiration.

the Government, under the supervision of the Navy Department. It has as its sole purpose the education and training of a limited number of young men of the country for careers as officers in the Naval Service. Obtaining an appointment to the Academy is a distinct triumph, but it is only an initial step, for there are many bridges to be crossed before you can become a full-fledged midshipman, as the students at the Naval Academy are called.

Every year the United States Government Printing Office, Washington, D. C., prints a pamphlet entitled: "Regulations governing the admission of candidates into the United States Naval Academy as Midshipmen and sample examination papers." The custodian of these publications is the Bureau of Navigation, Navy Department, and all communications relating to matters connected with the Naval Academy should be addressed to the chief of the Bureau of Navigation, Navy Department, Washington, D. C.

When you are considering a career as a naval officer, you should write for the latest of these pamphlets and sit down with your parents or, probably more effectively, with the family lawyer, and read its contents. It is very necessary that the instructions therein be thoroughly understood. Brief mention of what the pamphlet contains will be given in this book, merely for general information; but specific information on all topics given in the pamphlet must be studied.

The greater number of appointments to the Naval Academy are made by Senators, Representatives and Delegates from territories. Candidates to be eligible are required to reside in the congressional district of a Representative, the state of a Senator, or the territory of a Delegate. These legislators account for 2,655 appointments: five for each Senator, Representative or Delegate.

In addition, the Vice President is allowed five appointments; five are allowed from the District of Columbia from the residents of the District; and fifteen from the United States at large. It has become customary to make appointments at large from the sons of the officers and enlisted men of the regular Army, Navy and Marine Corps. The appointments at large and from the District of Columbia are made by the President, after competition in the regular entrance examination to the Naval Academy.

The Senators, Congressmen and Delegates have full control of the methods of making their appointments. For each principal appointment, an alternate appointment is also made. These alternates take the entrance examination at the same time as do the principals, and if a principal fails, a successful alternate will be available for the appointment.

The above are the means of obtaining appointments from civil life. Appointments to the Naval Academy from the regular Navy and Marine Corps also are authorized. One hundred enlisted men each year may be appointed, after a competitive examination, from those who can meet the age and physical requirements, and who measure up to the required standard of a prospective naval officer.

In addition to the above, the law authorizes the appointment, after competitive examination, of fifty enlisted men of the Naval Reserve or Marine Corps Reserve.

An additional forty young men can be appointed by the President from among the sons of the officers, soldiers, sailors, and marines of the Army, Navy, and Marine Corps, who were killed in action or died prior to July 2, 1921, of wounds in line of duty during the World War.

Twenty appointments from the honor graduates of honor schools designated by the War Department from members of the Naval Reserve Officers Training Corps Units can be made by the Secretary of the Navy.

Thus the chances for a young man to get an appointment are none too certain. But that is all the more reason why you should exert yourself—not only to obtain an appointment—but to prepare yourself studiously beforehand so you will not fail in the rigid examination. Once having become a midshipman, you must apply yourself thereafter, in order to complete the full course and receive a commission as an Ensign in the Navy.

Candidates who receive appointments should assure themselves before leaving home that they will measure up to the physical requirements. They should have themselves thoroughly examined by a competent physician—particularly regarding eyesight, color perception, hearing, kidney and heart trouble—and by a competent dentist for dental defects. Through such examinations any serious physical disqualification will be revealed, and the candidate spared the expense and trouble of a useless journey, and the disappointment of a rejection. Of course, such examinations cannot be conclusive, and will not affect the decision of the official examining boards.

All naval and recruiting stations to which medical

officers may be attached will give a preliminary examination to any candidate who has authority from a Senator or Representative to report for such examination. There are listed in the regulations governing the admission of candidates into the Naval Academy seventy-five naval and recruiting stations located in thirty-five states and the District of Columbia, where preliminary physical examinations will be held for candidates. But these examinations also are unofficial, and can in no way offset or take the place of the regular examination, which by law must be held by a board of medical examiners authorized to give regular physical examination before any candidate can enter the Naval Academy.

To show how urgent the Navy considers the necessity for candidates to take a preliminary examination, a warning is sounded in the above-mentioned pamphlet to those who would become naval officers, reading as follows:

"A sound body and constitution, suitable preparation, good natural capacity, an aptitude for study, industrious habits, perseverance, an obedient and orderly disposition, and a correct moral deportment, are such essential qualifications that the candidate knowingly deficient in any of these respects should not, as many do, subject themselves and their friends to the chances of future mortification and disappointment by accepting appointments to the Naval Academy, and entering on a career which they can not successfully pursue."

At the naval and recruiting stations there are officers, including medical officers, who are experienced in estimating the qualifications of young men, and who have a wide knowledge of human psychology, which enables them to estimate and advise candidates whether or not they are suitable material for the Navy.

A further warning is contained in the following paragraph in the same pamphlet of instructions to candidates:

"Candidates should not report for physical examination and admission to the Naval Academy, unless they are convinced by careful consideration of their personal and family circumstances that they will be satisfied to remain at the Naval Academy, complete the course, and accept commissions as Ensigns of the line, or such other commissions as may be offered in the United States Navy."

Candidates for appointment to the Naval Academy must be citizens of the United States not less than sixteen years of age nor more than twenty years of age on April first of the calendar year in which they enter the Naval Academy.

There are three ways of meeting the scholastic admission requirements open to those having outright nominations as principals and alternates, as follows: (1) by submitting acceptable certificates from an accredited secondary school, and from a university, college, or technical school of collegiate standing, accredited by the United States Naval Academy, and entering the Academy without examination; (2) by submitting acceptable certificates from a secondary school accredited by the United States Naval Academy, and passing a substantiating examination in English and mathematics; and (3) by passing the regular entrance examination in the following subjects: algebra, plane geometry, English composition and literature, United States history, ancient history, and physics.

Admission by either of the certified methods is a privilege which the Academic Board at the Naval Academy may accord those it considers, on the basis of the school records presented, to be capable of pursuing the Naval Academy course successfully. Candidates who fail to meet the certified requirements have a right to demonstrate their qualifications by passing the regular examinations.

Each candidate who has satisfied these requirements for admission to the Naval Academy must, before being admitted as a midshipman, make a deposit of $100. In addition to this deposit, the Government credits $250 to the account of each new midshipman. This $350 will be expended for uniforms, clothing, textbooks, etc. The $250 is considered an advance by the Government, and will be deducted from the midshipman's pay in monthly installments; or the midshipman may, immediately after entering the Academy, repay in full this amount of $250 from his own funds, and obviate the necessity of having the monthly deduction made from his pay. Midshipmen are paid $65 a month, or $780 a year, plus 75¢ a day as a ration allowance. While termed pay, this latter sum is, in effect, a maintenance allowance. This is furnished by the Government for the support of a midshipman during his preparation at the Naval Academy for service to be rendered after graduation upon being commissioned as an officer of the Navy. The ration allowance is almost always entirely used for the midshipman's board while he is in the Naval Academy. The $65 per month is utilized, under the direction of the superintendent of the Naval Academy, to provide such things as clothing and uniforms, textbooks and equipment, necessary toilet accessories, leave-money, and sundries.

When a midshipman graduates there will be a sum of money, compulsorily saved up for him out of his pay, to buy uniforms and clothing required on ceasing to be a midshipman. The balance unexpended is given to the midshipman upon graduation.

There will be no necessity for a midshipman to incur debt and no need for him to receive money from home. Midshipmen are expected to live within the limits of their pay.

In these days of early marriages it might be well to emphasize a rule which is contained in the regulations governing admission to the Naval Academy:

"No person who is married, or has been married, shall be admitted as a midshipman to the Naval Academy. Midshipmen shall not marry, and any midshipman found to be married shall be recommended for dismissal."

CHAPTER IV

QUALIFICATIONS NEEDED TO PASS THE ENTRANCE EXAMINATION TO THE NAVAL ACADEMY

MANY young men of our country who have felt the urge to be officers in the Navy, although physically capable of meeting the requirements of a stiff medical examination, often find themselves unable to pass the mental examination. They may even obtain the appointment from a Senator or a Representative, may pass the preliminary physical examination at one of the many naval and recruiting stations, practically assuring themselves of being capable of passing the regular physical examination before a board of medical examiners authorized to give such an examination, and then learn that their educational background is too elementary or inadequate, and that it is quite impossible for them to stand the mental examination for admission as a midshipman.

These mental examinations are held only twice a year, as follows: The first examination is held on the third Wednesday in February, the second on the third Wednesday in April, under the supervision of the Civil Service Commission, at certain places named, in all states of the Union, on a list given in the regulations governing the admission of candidates, already mentioned.

All those found mentally qualified in these examinations, who will be entitled to appointment in order of

Midshipmen marching to classes past another of the monuments dotting the campus, reminders of the importance of naval tradition.

Midshipmen studying in their quarters, plain but comfortable rooms. In caring for these quarters they learn the fundamental virtue of orderliness so important to the naval character.

It is apparent that these midshipmen are thoroughly enjoying this "Jackstay Drill," a lesson in knot-tying and splicing.

Before he becomes expert in nautical science, the midshipman must first learn to use the sailing instruments through practical instruction in navigation. Here a class is learning to take a sight of the sun with the sextant, an instrument used to determine a ship's position by the sun or stars.

nomination, will be notified by the Bureau of Navigation when to report to the Naval Academy for physical examination, and if qualified in this examination will be appointed as midshipmen.

It has been demonstrated that it is most beneficial for the candidates who are preparing themselves for the Naval Academy entrance examination to take a refresher course at one of the well-recognized preparatory schools for at least six months before their examination. In the Naval Academy examination a time limit is placed upon the examination in each subject; for instance, a two-hour written examination is prescribed each in United States history, physics, and English composition and literature, and three hours each for the examinations in algebra and geometry. Preparatory schools recognize that even though the youth may know the correct answers to examination questions, unless they have been practiced in telling their knowledge within the time limit allowed, they may be incapable of completing enough questions to obtain the passing mark of 2.5, or 62½ per cent. These schools have established a practice of obtaining many sample sets of Naval Academy examinations of previous years, and periodically hold trial examinations in writing of their candidate students, with the object of training them to write down in a minimum time correct answers to all the questions. Without this training, many young men, even with ample knowledge, often fail to complete the Naval Academy examinations.

A young man cannot start too early to prepare himself mentally for the examination to the Naval Academy, and also to acquire the basic knowledge and studious habits needed if he is to become a midshipman and successfully complete the difficult course of study prescribed there. Many apply, but few are chosen. A youth must make up his mind early to be one of the successful.

Candidates who do not submit acceptable certificates will be examined mentally in English composition and literature. United States history, algebra (through quadratics and including the progressions and the binomial theorem, elementary theory of logarithms and numerical trigonometry, the use of the sine, cosine and tangent in solving right triangles), plane geometry, (five books), solid geometry (three books), and physics (one year's work). Deficiency in any one of these subjects will be sufficient to insure the rejection of the candidate.

Commencing with the entrance examinations of 1941, chemistry will be added to the subjects comprising the regular entrance examinations. The subject matter in general will embrace the topics of the standard first-year high school course in chemistry.

The attention of the young men who are preparing themselves for the examinations is especially invited to the above-mentioned regulations governing the admission of candidates, under the subject, "General Character of the Regular Examinations," as follows:

English composition and literature—This examination, which presupposes three years' study of English in a secondary school, conforms to the general requirements set by the College Entrance Examination Board. In particular, it is planned to test the candidate's fitness to undertake English work in the Academy. Consequently no paper in English or in history, however accurate it may be in subject matter, will be regarded as satisfactory if seriously deficient in paragraphing, sentence structure, punctuation, spelling, or other essentials of good usage.

The examination will consist of questions in grammar, composition, and literature. For questions in literature, the Naval Academy no longer prescribes a list of books upon which preparation should be made, but leaves the choice to the candidate, with the recommendation that he read and study works of recognized excellence in each of the following groups: (1) drama, (2) prose narrative, (3) poetry, (4) essays, biographies, and miscellaneous prose. Accordingly, the test will be not of the candidate's knowledge of specially designated books, but of his ability to discuss "his reading intelligently, with adequate scope, and with a usable knowledge of elementary critical terms." It is important that he should have an acquaintance "with traditionally great literature and with recognized literary types."

United States history—The examination in this branch may include questions concerning the early settlements in this country; the forms of government in the Colonies; the causes, leading events, and the results of wars; territorial expansion and industrial growth, including map studies; the Constitution of the United States; the policy of the United States in foreign affairs, tariff, currency, trusts, labor, immigration, and other present-day problems; and the lives and public service of great Americans.

Algebra—The examination in algebra will include questions and problems upon the fundamental operations, factoring, fractions, the meaning and use of formulas, graphical representation, linear equations, simplification of expressions involving surds, the solution and theory of quadratic equations, problems involving the formation of simple and quadratic equations, exponents, radicals, elementary theory and use of logarithms, variation, progressions, binomial theorem for positive integral exponents, the solution of simple types of equations of degree higher than the second numerical trigonometry—the use of the sine, cosine, and tangent in solving right triangles.

Geometry—The examination in geometry will cover the standard propositions in plane and solid geometry and their use in the solution of numerical problems. Candidates will be required to demonstrate propositions, including original theorems and loci problems, and to solve original exercises by construction or computation.

Physics—The examination will be based on the topics listed under the certificate requirements. No laboratory work will be required, but some of the questions will be based on subject matter of which the candidate will have better knowledge from having performed experiments. Approximately half of the examination will consist of simple problems based upon the subject matter of the requirements. The candidate will be required to know the following physical constants: Conversion factors from English to metric system (2.2 lbs/kgm.; 39.37 in./m.); density of mercury (13.6 gm./cm^3); acceleration due to gravity (32.2 ft./sec.^{2}, 980 cm/sec.^{2}); density of water (62.4 lbs./ft.^{3}); value of horsepower (550 ft.-lbs./sec., 746 watts); melting and boiling points of water; absolute zero (—273° C.); heat of fusion of ice (80 cal./gm.); heat of vaporization of water (539 cal./gm.);

mechanical equivalent of heat (778 ft.-lbs./B. t. u.); speed of sound at 0° C. (1,087 ft./sec.).

Although an attempt has been made in this chapter to give you a more intimate acquaintance with the initial step in the process of how to be a naval officer, that does not relieve those who want to enter the naval life as officers, from the necessity of obtaining the publications pertaining to the Naval Academy which will be sent them on application by the Bureau of Navigation, Navy Department, Washington, D. C., and studying the entire publication from cover to cover.

I have often heard inquiries made as to why the examination for the Naval Academy was made so difficult, and why so many young men failed to pass.

The answer is that the Naval Academy is a Government School. The cost of a midshipman's education is borne by the United States Treasury. The expense runs into high figures. The Government wishes to be certain that those who enter as midshipmen will be capable of finishing the four years course. Every young man who fails to graduate is a money loss to the Government.

The entrance examinations are created in order to give in each case a definite idea of the candidate's mental calibre. The examination in English Composition and Literature will show whether the candidate has applied himself and has attained basic mental training in order to continue successfully like studies at the Naval Academy. The history examination tests his basic knowledge and his facility to interpret and explain what he has learned of the life of his country.

The examination in mathematics likewise tests his

grounding in that science which is at the foundation of all the scientific studies which he will meet later at the Academy.

Physics test his knowledge of the natural laws governing physical phenomena cause and effect, met in everyday life and assure a foundation for the higher physics taught at the Academy.

The candidate who successfully passes these examinations can be reasonably sure of being able to understand and master the intricate course which will give him the mental training and knowledge necessary for an officer in the Navy.

CHAPTER V

THE HISTORY AND PURPOSE OF THE NAVAL ACADEMY

THE United States Naval Academy at Annapolis, Maryland, is the only national educational college in this country where duly appointed young men are educated and trained to become officers of the *line* of the Navy of the United States. The *line* is the executive branch, distinct from staff branches. The students of the Naval Academy are appointed by the Navy Department as midshipmen, and are considered as a part of the regular Navy. They are neither officers nor enlisted men, but they hold a position of social equality with the officers.

The basic principle underlying a military education, such as is followed at the Naval Academy, is not only to impart an academic and scientific education and training to the students, but also to develop in them the important attributes of self-reliance, manliness, orderliness and neatness, correct social behavior, polite manners, respect for law and order, coöperation, and patriotism. The aim of the Naval Academy training is to create in each of the graduates a high sense of duty, and to develop the highest type of American citizens.

In a university or a college, the young men attending are trained primarily for civil pursuits. Therefore such institutions are places of opportunity. The Naval Academy is a place of obligation.

Midshipmen are sworn to uphold and defend the Constitution of the United States. They voluntarily assume the obligation to perform certain duties, and, if need be, lay down their lives in the country's defense.

It must be clearly understood that all who enter the Naval Service by that act lay aside certain rights and privileges which independent citizens are free to exercise. Among the rights surrendered by naval men are the freedom to go and come at will, and the right to question or discuss the official acts and orders of the senior officers set over them according to law.

The United States Navy discipline is built on the recognizedly advantageous procedure of arousing an individual's pride, and on the human incentive to excel in any undertaking, rather than on the fear of punishment. Behind this method is the objective of stimulating a high sense of honor, personal responsibility, reliability, and trustworthiness.

The title "midshipman" is derived from the ancient term, "amidships man." In the days when warships were propelled by sail, "amidships men" were employed to transmit orders between the high decks, forward and aft, on board the great high-walled wooden ships of the line. At first, these "amidships men" were elderly seamen. In time they were replaced by active boys and young men, and because the passing of orders accurately was so important in battle or in maneuvers, the status of the "amidships men" became that of young officers. These positions were sought after by young gentlemen of birth and breeding. By the beginning of the eighteenth century these young officers had been given the title of "mid-

Although the ensign who wants to specialize in aviation must subsequently go to the school at Pensacola, certain fundamentals of aviation are taught at the Academy. This midshipman is learning to use the aerial machine-gun.

"Middies" at Annapolis take a course in cutter handling.

In training patrol planes anchored on the Severn River, midshipmen acquire additional basic knowledge of naval aviation.

Courses at the Naval Academy are three-fold: lectures, recitations, and practical instruction. This is a lecture course in electrical science.

Lecture course in marine engineering, supplemented by practical demonstrations.

Laboratory work in steam engineering, in which the midshipmen acquire a first-hand knowledge of the modern fighting ship's power plant.

A lecture course in mathematics, on which the future officer's entire structure of knowledge is based. Without algebra, geometry, and calculus, he cannot attain proficiency in gunnery, navigation, or any of the other branches of naval science.

Even a practical knowledge of boat-building is essential to the Navy officer's complete education, for although he may never be called upon to repair a boat, he must be prepared for any possibility.

shipmen," and the grade became the preliminary step in the life of a naval officer.

In 1845, the Secretary of the Navy was George Bancroft of Massachusetts. During his term of office the Naval School of the United States was established at Annapolis. Bancroft was a statesman, scholar, historian, and an experienced school administrator and organizer. It was because of his firm convictions on the necessity for proper education, that this institution was established to give our young sea officers a basic foundation in the elements of their profession. The course at first was five years, of which the first and last were spent at the Naval School. The other three were passed at sea.

In 1850, the name was changed from the Naval School to the United States Naval Academy. A year later the course was made four years of consecutive study, with practice cruises in warships during the summer. This is the rule today.

When steam machinery was introduced in warships, the need for engineer officers caused the introduction of two courses of study: one for midshipmen preparing to be line officers, and the other for those expecting to become engineer officers. In 1899, the line course and the engineering courses were merged; then all midshipmen were given a rigid course of study not only in the elements of study of the line, such as navigation, ordnance, gunnery, and so forth, but also in both marine and electrical engineering. The naval officer of the line from that time has been expected not only to sail, navigate, and fight naval ships, but also to operate the steam machinery of the vessels.

After the war between the States the naval hero, Admiral D. D. Porter, was made superintendent of the Naval Academy. He had begun his naval career at the age of eleven, while serving in his father's naval ship. This young man had fought the pirates in the Caribbean. In the war between the States, he had been a famous leader of the Union Navy. He rose in rank from a lieutenant in 1861 to a rear admiral in 1863. As superintendent, he was responsible for many excellent reforms in the treatment of the midshipmen. He inaugurated the honor system, under which the midshipmen no longer were treated as boys, but as men to be trusted, so long as they merited the confidence placed in them.

Today, as then, the head of the Naval Academy is the Superintendent, a Rear Admiral on the active list of the Navy, who receives his orders directly from the Bureau of Navigation, under which bureau of the Navy Department the Naval Academy is administered. The next senior in rank is the Commandant of Midshipmen, usually a Captain in the Navy; as the executive officer under the Superintendent, he is head of the Executive Department. There are nine other departments, each with a head, usually a Commander or Captain in the Navy. The Superintendent, the Commandant of Midshipmen, and the heads of the nine other departments form the Academic Board.

The old Naval Academy consisted of a rambling assortment of buildings, following no uniform pattern of architectural design. In 1889 the designs for a new Naval Academy were provided, money appropriated, and additional grounds purchased by Congress. Today we have a splendidly equipped Naval Academy, handsomely constructed, covering an area of one hundred and eighty-four acres, and representing an investment of about thirty million dollars. In addition to the Naval Academy grounds proper, commonly called the "yard," are the hospital grounds of twenty-two acres immediately adjoining, with an up-to-date hospital; a rifle range across the Severn River of one hundred and fifty-one acres; and a dairy farm of eight hundred and fifty-five acres, about thirteen miles from Annapolis. It is a happy day for the aspiring naval officer when he finds he has received his appointment as a midshipman and walks for the first time through the bronze portals of the Main Gate of the Academy. He is entering the place that will be his home for the next four years, except when he is at sea, a place in which the best traditions of our Navy are concentrated. He will probably stop for a moment between the guns, captured by the Navy during the war with Mexico, that flank the chapel and read on the handsome chapel doors the Latin motto by which he will henceforth live: "Non Sibi Patria—Not for Self but for Country."

There, actually on the grounds for the first time, he will begin to appreciate the true spirit of the Navy—to see how strong is the bond between the present and the past. To quote from the admirable pen-picture of the Academy prepared by the Bureau of Navigation, "Every monument, every flag, every trophy, every memorial, even the names of the buildings in which the midshipmen live and work, the walks they tread, and the fields in which they drill or engage in sports—all are constant reminders of the worthy service and glorious deeds of naval officers who have preceded them, and at the same time are incentives to high endeavor and ambitious emulation."

To the outsider some of the traditions may seem merely amusing, but they are all expressions of a strong unity. Even the smallest traditions at the Academy are important: the Japanese Bell, given to Commodore M. C. Perry when he landed on the Lew Chew Islands during his famous expedition to Japan, which the midshipmen ring only in celebration of a football victory over their traditional rival, West Point; Tecumseh, the bronze replica of the original figurehead of the frigate *Delaware* which the midshipmen salute enroute to examinations to insure a passing mark of 2.5, and who has therefore come to be known familiarly as "The God of 2.5".

There are other traditions, some frivolous, some glorious, but all important. Without them a Navy is like a rudderless ship without a compass to direct it. They are all clung to tenaciously; they are the Navy's shield and buckler. Traditions of heroic service have become our guiding genius—confessions of faith, examples to be emulated by every officer and man of the Navy. High traditions give men the strength to stay to the last, to go down if they must, but with their colors still nailed to the mast. Traditions give added courage to the brave and turn timidity into fearlessness.

Then there are the traditions of the Naval Service—not as inspiring as those born in battle—but equally significant: the traditions of discipline that regulate the relation of the officer to the enlisted man; the reverence for rank; a high ideal of duty; the Navy's efficiency above all else; and a jealous resistance against unskilled domination. These beliefs have been handed down through successive generations of officers and men. The officers, being the more permanent and of necessity the more highly educated, have been the guardians of these traditions. There is no safe passport to high place in the Naval Service save virtue and wisdom.

I can remember still the words of Edmund Burke, impressed upon us at the Naval Academy when I was a midshipman nearly fifty years ago. They were: "Everything ought to be open, but not indifferently, to every man. No rotation, no appointment by lot, no mode of election operating in the spirit of sortition or rotation. The road to eminence and power from obscure conditions ought not to be easy. If rare merit be the rarest of all rare things, it ought to pass through some sort of probation. The temple of honor ought to be seated on an eminence. If it be opened through virtue, let it be remembered, too, that virtue is never tried but by some difficulty and some struggle."

CHAPTER VI

LIFE AT THE NAVAL ACADEMY

THE midshipmen, over 2,500 strong, are organized
into a regiment of four battalions, each battalion composed of three companies. The battalions are supervised
by experienced commissioned officers of the Navy. The
regiment is officered throughout all its units by midshipmen of the first or senior class.

The regular commissioned officer leaders of the battalions are charged with the administration of discipline
in their unit, also instruct their midshipmen in the
principles of leadership and the elements affecting
morale, including personal finance. These officers make
it their duty to know personally every midshipman under
them, and advise them.

The regiment of midshipmen is grouped scholastically
into four classes. The members of the fourth class are
called "plebes," and correspond to "freshmen" at the
civilian colleges. The reader must bear in mind that the
term "fourth class," applies to the midshipmen in their
first year. From then on, the classes are numbered con-
secutively, in reverse order, the next higher being the
third class; the next, the second class; and the last, or
graduating class, the first class.

Bancroft Hall, where the midshipmen live, has four
wings. In each wing is quartered one battalion. The midshipmen recite only with members of their own class,
but outside of class work they are administered as a military organization.

The courses of study are distributed among ten departments: Executive; Seamanship and Navigation; Ordnance and Gunnery; Marine Engineering; Mathematics; Electrical Engineering; English, History and Government; Languages; Hygiene; and Physical Training. These will be described later.

Twenty-two per cent of the academic work is devoted to professional subjects; 51 per cent to mathematics and the sciences, pure and applied; and 27 per cent to other subjects.

The new fourth class enters the Academy each year during early summer. During the first three months these novices are given practical instruction in infantry, in boat handling, and on the rifle range. During these months a lecture and reading course is given them, supervised by the Department of English History and Government.

In September, the last months before the scholastic year commences, the fourth class midshipmen receive instructions in preliminary academic work to familiarize them with Naval Academy methods of recitation and study.

The academic year commences about the first of October, and continues to the last of May, with almost no interruption except for a few days of leave granted at Christmas time.

Midshipmen are divided by classes into sections for recitation purposes. Individual marks are assigned at each day's recitation in all subjects. Four times a year, at the end of a two-month period, examinations are held in all subjects, and marks given, ranging from 0 to 4. The passing mark is 2.5, which corresponds to a 62½ per cent mark on a 100 per cent rating. In the event of failure in any subject for the term consisting of four months, a midshipman may be turned back into the next lower class, or his resignation from the Naval Service requested.

After the completion of the first academic year, the midshipmen of the fourth class become third classmen, and embark in a squadron of battleships for a summer cruise.

During this cruise these third classmen perform the work on board ship habitually performed by naval ratings or enlisted men. They scrub the decks, fire the boilers, steer the ship, operate machinery of all kinds, and make themselves familiar with the various phases and intricacies of the life of a sailorman at sea. Every day during the cruise these young men receive practical instructions in gunnery, navigation, seamanship, electrical engineering, marine engineering, and radio. All instruction is supplemented by lectures. Before disembarking at the end of a practice cruise, the midshipmen of all classes on board hold a target practice, firing both the turret guns and the smaller guns of the battleships.

After completing the second academic year, the third class becomes the second class. The second class does not take the summer practice cruise, but remains at the Naval Academy during the summer to be given practical instruction in aviation, engineering, navigation, and seamanship. The midshipmen of the second class also are given a month's coastal cruise in destroyers during the summer.

After completing the third academic year, the second class becomes the first class. The new first class then

"Shove off number one!" The command is barked out and the midshipmen are away for a cutter-drill on the Severn, acquiring skill in boat handling, and developing teamwork. It's also good exercise.

With sailboats in the foreground, a division of destroyers are seen moored together, ready to take the midshipmen on their summer practice cruises to the Caribbean or perhaps through the Panama Canal to Hawaii.

Achievement of military bearing among midshipmen is no hit-and-miss matter.
Known as a "posture machine," this device records the faults of the entering
midshipman and charts his subsequent progress.

Midshipmen aboard a battleship ready to embark on a practice cruise.

A replica of the figurehead of the USS *Delaware*, known familiarly to the midshipmen as "Tecumseh"—a variation of the name of the Delaware Indian chief represented. A penny tossed to Tecumseh on the way to an examination is supposed to assure a passing mark.

Not all drill at the Academy is on the water. Here the midshipmen are engaged in infantry drill, developing skill in marching and the manual of arms.

The old adage concerning all work and no play applies at the Naval Academy as elsewhere. The competitive spirit in athletics is encouraged and the Varsity teams meet leading university teams in all sports. Above, on the home field at Annapolis, the midshipmen (and the Navy goat) watch a touchdown play.

Lacrosse, a game not widely played in this country, is popular with the budding ensigns. It's a fast, grueling game in which their stout hearts are put to the test.

One of the most picturesque sights at the Academy occurs when the midshipmen are out on the Severn for a sailboat drill, in which they get a feel for the water and wind and put into practice some of the basic principles of seamanship.

On Saturday nights basketball gives way to the fox-trot as the Academy gymnasium becomes the scene of a gala "hop," with the midshipmen in full dress and their best girls in brilliant formal costumes.

The USS *Chicago*, one of the six heavy cruisers launched in 1929 and 1930, weighing 9,300 tons, carrying a complement of 611 officers and men, and armed with 8-inch, 5-inch anti-aircraft, and machine guns. Torpedo tubes were removed in 1935 and additional anti-aircraft guns mounted.

A scene on Academy lawn at the end of the academic year in June as prizes and trophies of various sorts are awarded to midshipmen outstanding in studies, athletics, and military deportment.

The end of one trail—and the beginning of another. Graduation exercises at the Academy in June as the midshipmen receive their degrees and diplomas and become ensigns. In a month they will all be with the fleet.

The USS Portland and her complement of planes in the air. These planes serve as scouts for the warship, assist in range-finding and report results of gun-fire. They are launched from catapults, land on the sea, and are then hauled back on board with the crane visible on the fore-deck.

leaves for the summer practice cruise, but the duties this time are different than on the third class cruise. Now the midshipmen's duties conform closely to those of commissioned officers.

Midshipmen of the first and third classes are granted a month's leave on the return from the battleship cruise in the latter part of August. Those of the second class obtain their month's leave after completing their summer work at the Academy and the destroyer cruise.

In order to economize the time of midshipmen, and to give the greatest possible amount of instruction, careful schedules are followed during the four years' course. Throughout each academic year, the midshipman's life is governed by a carefully prepared schedule. His day—from the beginning of the scholastic year until its end—starts at 6:20 A.M., when reveille is sounded with the bugle and electric bells. Forty seconds after the first note of reveille, room inspection is begun. All doors are opened, and an occupant of each room reports "all out" as the reveille inspectors double time along the corridors. The "all out" means that the occupants of the room (two or three midshipmen) are up, the bedclothes thrown over the foot of the bed, and the mattresses turned back.

Twenty-five minutes are allowed for the morning shower, shave and dressing. Breakfast formation is at 6:45 A.M. During the formation the daily orders are read, and the midshipmen are inspected by midshipmen officers or commissioned officers, who note their general appearances, and award demerits if their shoes and uniforms are not well brushed, and the midshipmen themselves are not in neat condition.

Immediately after inspection, the regiment is marched to breakfast, where the midshipmen take their assigned places, twenty-one at each table. Following the breakfast, morning prayers are read by the Chaplain. After prayers, the midshipmen return to their rooms to make up their beds, sweep, dust, and put things in order.

At 7:45 A.M., half the regiment marches to its first recitation, while the other half commences its study hour. During the week, Monday through Friday, the academic day is divided into six periods of approximately one hour each, with four periods during the forenoon—two for study, and two for recitations.

Lunch formation is at 12:20 P.M., and again the midshipmen are inspected while the orders are being published. At 1:10 P.M., the fifth recitation period commences, and this is followed for some battalions by long afternoon drills and for the others by the sixth recitation period and short drills.

The afternoon drills are completed at 4:10 P.M. or 4:30 P.M., and from then until dinner formation at 6:40 P.M. the midshipmen, except those on duty on each floor of Bancroft Hall, engage in athletics or other non-scholastic activities.

On Wednesday a short drill is held, usually followed by a dress parade. On Saturday there are two recitation periods and two drill periods during the afternoon, followed by rigid personal inspection of the regiment on the regimental parade, or by an equally thorough room inspection, if the weather does not permit an outdoor formation. On Saturday afternoon all midshipmen, except those on duty or those having extra duty to perform, are permitted to visit the city of Annapolis. On Saturday afternoon there are always athletic events, depending upon the season. On Saturday evenings there are usually dances, motion pictures, or dramatic and musical entertainments.

On Sundays and holidays reveille is at 7:15 A.M. Church attendance is compulsory, the midshipmen being permitted to attend either the Naval Academy Chapel or a church of their own denomination in Annapolis. On Sunday afternoon the midshipmen, except fourth class, are permitted to visit the city. After the evening meal the midshipmen are permitted half an hour leisure before the evening study period commences. This begins at 8 P.M. and continues until 9:50 P.M. At 10 o'clock tattoo is sounded, and five minutes later the notes of taps mark the end of the midshipmen's day and "lights out."

Life at the Naval Academy today does not fundamentally differ from the time when I was a midshipman nearly fifty years ago. The corps of midshipmen then consisted of 250, grouped into one battalion of four companies. Our studies were less scientific than those today. Modern engineering and electricity were still in swaddling clothes. Radio had not been discovered. Our practice cruises were taken in sailing ships such as the old *Constitution* and the *Constellation*. Midshipmen were trained to go aloft and furl sail to heights of 125 feet from the deck with nothing to hold on to but shrouds and foot ropes. That was in the twilight zone, during the transition from sail to steam. The conservative men of the sea, while adopting the inventions of steam and electricity, still held on to sail, for fear the new fangled means of propulsion would fail them in a time of emergency.

CHAPTER VII

COURSES OF STUDY AT THE NAVAL ACADEMY

IN THE half century since I entered the Academy as a midshipman the fundamental traits demanded of an officer have not changed, but there have been revolutionary developments in the field of naval science—particularly as it has been affected by mechanical improvements. Once a fighting ship's equipment consisted of stout sail, a stout crew, several howitzers, bolted as firmly as possible to the deck, and a good wind. Whereas ships once fought hand to hand, a modern battleship may now fire upon an adversary lying below the horizon line. I sometimes wonder what John Paul Jones would think if he could step onto today's fighting ship. As you know, if you have ever visited one even briefly, it is complex and bewildering.

Considering this, you will see that the course of study at the Academy today has a two-fold purpose: (1) to train future officers in the changeless essentials of military character and in naval tactics; (2) to train future officers to supervise and coordinate the manifold operations necessary to keep a modern warship in the pink of condition, as ready to respond to the will of the captain as does the human to the will of its owner.

Naturally, no officer is capable of unifying a group of specialized operations unless he himself thoroughly understands each of these operations. On board a modern

battleship are a thousand or so men of assorted specialties. They are divided into branches according to the
work they perform.

One branch is the "seaman branch." The officers of
this branch are called line officers. This branch handles
the ship and fights the guns. Their specialty is that of
the pure sailorman. All of them work above deck. The
higher ratings of the men in this branch are the boatswain's mates, turret captains, gun captains, quarter-
masters, gunner's mates, sailmaker's mates, etc.

The next branch is the "artificer branch," comprising
men who repair the structure of the ship and its hull
fittings. Among the specialists here are the carpenter's
mates, ship fitters, plumbers, painters, blacksmiths, cop-
persmiths, etc.

The engineer's branch has control of the boilers and
engines, also the electrical installation of the ship. Among
the ratings are machinist's mates, electricians (both general and for radio or wireless), oilers, boilermakers, water
tenders, and firemen.

The special branch includes the non-technical ratings,
men whose trades fall in the non-combatant type, such
as yeomen or clerks, hospital corps men, cooks, messmen,
etc.

These ratings include a diversified lot of skills and in
order to weld them all together the future officer must
first have training in each of the specialties themselves
and then training in coordination. When he leaves the
Academy as an ensign, he knows a fighting ship from
top to bottom.

His military instruction is given by the Executive
Department defined in Chapter V. This department has

charge of the development of officerlike character, including the qualities of initiative, attention to duty, military bearing, cleanliness of mind and person, neatness of dress, and aptitude for the service. This instruction includes an all-important course in leadership.

Other instruction is divided roughly into nine groups: Seamanship and Navigation; Ordnance and Gunnery; Marine Engineering; Mathematics; Electrical Engineering; English, History, and Government; Languages; Hygiene; Physical Training.

Each of these studies has a definite contribution to make in the creation of a forceful, competent naval officer. So that you, as a prospective midshipman, will have a general idea of the scope of each, and so that you may judge for yourself your ability to pursue the four-year course, brief descriptions follow. A more detailed analysis of the courses will be found in the appendix.

SEAMANSHIP AND NAVIGATION. Just as the first function of an infantryman is to know how to walk, the first function of a cavalryman to ride a horse, the first function of a naval officer is to know how to sail his ship in good order. It is a complex study, but one that is endlessly fascinating for anyone who has the sea in his blood. It includes the fundamentals of tactics, communications, aviation, military law, the regulations and customs of the Navy. When completed, it gives the midshipman a sound foundation for future study of these subjects.

ORDNANCE AND GUNNERY. The second function of a Navy man is know how to fight the guns. His ship is his floating fort, to be maneuvered into position—to be in the right place at the right time. His guns are his mailed fists by which he makes his presence felt. In this course the midshipman learns to make the most effective use of every weapon at the command of a modern navy—pistols, machine guns, rifles, anti-aircraft guns, landing guns, torpedoes, the big guns, and even chemicals. Throughout the course great stress is laid not only on the duties of officers in gunnery, but the relations of each subject to the development of ordnance and gunnery in the United States Navy, the present gunnery methods of the fleet, and the future problems which may be met by the naval officer.

MARINE ENGINEERING. Even as an aviator must be thoroughly familiar with all the mechanical mysteries of his craft to fly it and fight it efficiently, so must the naval officer know every brass screw on his ship. Here the midshipman is instructed in mechanical engineering, warship construction, damage control and all the other subjects which will fit him, upon graduation, to perform intelligently and efficiently such duties as may be assigned to him involving any of the elements of the naval profession concerning mechanical engineering and ship structure.

MATHEMATICS. The importance to the naval officer of a thorough training in mathematics should be obvious. Unless he is at home in algebra, trigonometry, and calculus, his whole structure of knowledge—including his knowledge of tactics and gunnery—will topple to the ground.

ELECTRICAL ENGINEERING. Warfare today—particularly naval warfare—depends less and less upon the individual combatant's strong right arm and more and more upon that small but powerful spark which Benjamin Franklin drew out of the sky with a kite. Electricity in many ways is the life-blood of a battleship. Coupled with radio, it comprises the eyes and ears of a modern navy. Here the midshipman learns not only the basic science of electricity but the companion sciences of chemistry and physics.

ENGLISH, HISTORY, AND GOVERNMENT. Unlike some other military organizations, the military organization of the United States does not believe its officers can attain full efficiency if they are mere automatons. It believes its naval officers should be gentlemen in the fullest sense of the word. The emphasis placed in this department on such subjects as literature and after-dinner speaking may seem surprising to you, but their importance is great. A naval officer is a representative of his country. He is, wherever he goes—China, Chile, or Timbuktu—an emissary of the United States. In some portions of the world he is almost the only United States citizen with which the natives come in contact. He must be articulate; for as a leader he must be able to communicate his orders and ideas forcefully. He can never advance in his profession unless his tools are sharp. A study of history helps to develop what we have called his trained initiative. A study of government gives him an understanding and appreciation of the country whose safety is in his hands. In studying naval history he becomes familiar with all the tactical coups and blunders of the past, and adds them to his own experience; furthermore, seeing the history of the navy as a whole, he sees his job more clearly, adds the courage of past heroes to his own, accepts the honorable trust that has been handed down to him.

The *Skipjack*, one of the Navy's more modern submarines—an underwater craft designed to achieve maximum speed, fighting strength, surface cruising range, and underwater stamina. It displaces 1,450 tons, is 298 feet long, and carries one 3-inch anti-aircraft gun on the aft deck in addition to its six 21-inch torpedo tubes. The average submarine carries a complement of between fifty and sixty-five officers and men.

In addition to its underwater service, a submarine must be able to protect itself on the surface. Therefore it carries one or two anti-aircraft guns on the deck, usually 3-inch, but sometimes 4-inch or even 6-inch weapons. Here a crew is serving, or loading, one of the guns.

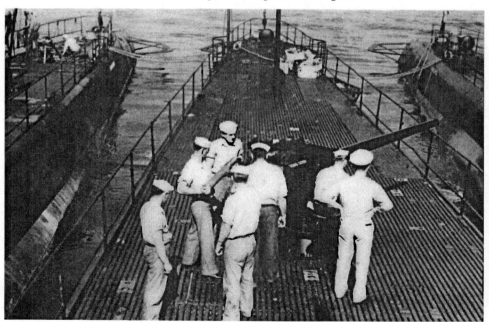

One of the most hazardous of all Navy jobs is diving. But it is a job of great importance not only to the operation of submarines but to the whole fleet. This grotesquely outfitted diver is ready to descend for rescue or repair work. The rope attached on the front is his descending line. The line attached to the rear of the helmet is the tube through which he receives oxygen.

To work efficiently, a diver must be in constant communication with the surface. Here, just before putting on his helmet to descend, the telephone is being tested.

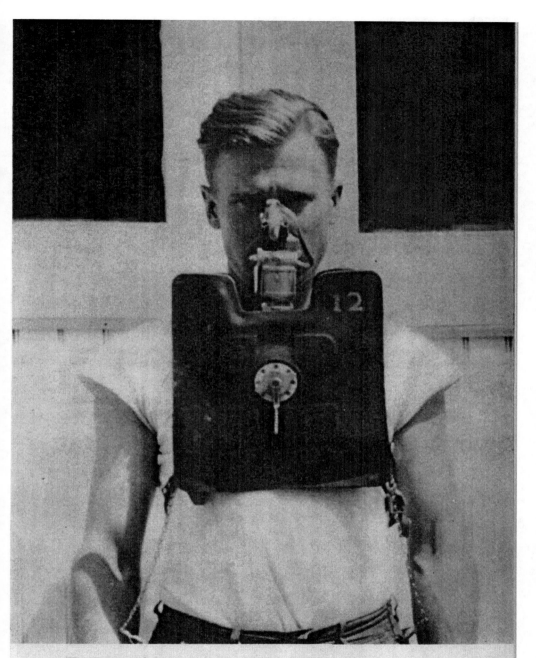

The danger of being trapped in a disabled submarine has been considerably lessened since the invention of the Momsen Lung, known to men in the service simply as "The Lung." Wearing the device as shown in this picture, a man may leave a submarine at a considerable depth via the escape hatch and rise slowly to the surface without ill-effects from the great change in air-pressure.

Cadets entering a training plane with their instructor at the United States Naval Air Station at Pensacola, Florida, where ensigns are trained for service in the air branch of the fleet.

A group of young aviation students at Pensacola study the octant—a celestial navigation instrument which corresponds to the sextant used on shipboard for reckoning by the sun and stars.

LANGUAGES. In the Navy, as in the diplomatic service, there must be a large number of officers capable of acting as interpreters of the various languages encountered in line of duty abroad—French, Spanish, German, and Italian. The basic language studies add to the midshipman's general culture and when he has completed the course, if he desires, he may have the opportunity of qualifying as a naval interpreter.

HYGIENE. As Napoleon pointed out, "an army travels on its stomach." He might also have added that a navy's officers must be as fit as the guns they are firing. The officers of our Navy are as fit a group of men as one will find anywhere in the world. Their profession is conducive to fitness. The aim of this course is to keep them that way, to train future officers to keep their bodily equipment in tip-top shape during peace and under all the adverse conditions they may meet in time of war.

PHYSICAL TRAINING. Hand in hand with the course in hygiene goes the Academy's course in physical training. Since he spends his life on the water, a naval officer naturally must be a strong swimmer and expert in all forms of life-saving. Strength and military posture are the main objectives of the course, but the Academy believes that in acquiring these the midshipman is entitled to the excitement of competitive sports. The top-ranking Varsity teams of the Academy compete, as you know, with universities, colleges, and preparatory schools. Within the Academy itself, the wide range of competitive sports assures practically every midshipman of participating in one or more branches during his four-year course. The emphasis throughout is on good sportsmanship, one of the essential qualities of military character.

These are merely the barest outlines of the courses of study at the Academy. All of them are supplemented as the midshipman chooses by reading in the splendid Academy library, stocked with more than 86,000 volumes of all subjects and growing at the rate of almost 2,000 volumes a year. You may be sure, the next time you meet an officer in our Navy, that he is not only a trained fighting man but an athlete and a scholar.

CHAPTER VIII

FROM THE ACADEMY TO THE
FLEET—PROMOTION

Each June a stirring scene takes place as the members of the first class in shining full-dress march for the last time down Stribling Walk and, at the end of the graduation exercises, give out a mighty cheer as they throw their midshipmen's caps high into the air. That cheer is a lusty expression of triumph, always thrilling after the gravity of the ceremonies, and the graduating men have it coming to them. It is a release, for they have worked hard—and successfully. The caps thrown aloft are symbolic: the men who were plebes four years ago are now ensigns. They're in the Navy now.

Suppose, for a moment, that you have fulfilled your four-year's course at the Academy, taken your place among the men of the first class, received your diploma, and the degree of Bachelor of Science, and with the rest of them flung your midshipman's cap to the four winds. You stand for a moment in the bedlam of cheering and congratulations. What happens to the new ensign now?

First of all, he is given a month's leave. Then (unless he has applied for and been granted a commission in the Marine Corps, which will be discussed later), he will report for duty to some vessel of the fleet, where he will take up his shipboard duties. These are many and varied. In the beginning, he will serve in the gunnery department of the ship as a junior officer of a gun division. Here he will gain experience in supervising enlisted personnel, in drilling them in the turrets or in the broadside batteries. After some time in the gunnery department, the ensign is transferred to the engineering department. After this period he goes to the communication division where he learns naval radio and signal methods.

The young officer soon grows accustomed to positions of responsibility that involve the safety of both men and ships; he is further developing his initiative and sound judgment—without which no one can long remain an officer in the Navy.

Two years after graduation he becomes eligible for either aviation or submarine duty. The procedure in these branches will be discussed in the next Chapter.

Three years after graduation, provided he remains with the surface fleet and meets all requirements, the ensign is promoted to the rank of lieutenant, junior grade. After another year at sea he becomes eligible for postgraduate instruction ashore, or for duty at one of the various navy yards or naval stations.

Naturally, as an officer advances in experience and rank, he is assigned duties of greater and greater responsibility. On board one of the big surface ships at sea he becomes, in turn, a division officer, then head of one of the several departments on board ship—such as gunnery officer, navigator, senior engineer—and then executive officer or, in other words, second in command of the ship, and finally commanding officer. Eventually, when advanced to the grade of rear admiral, the highest rank in our Navy, he is given command of a detachment consisting of several warships. The ultimate ambition of all line officers, of course, is to command the entire fleet.

In any military organization such as the Navy, the large foundation group of subordinate officers must be assured of advancement through successive steps to higher ranks, where responsibility and authority are proportionally increased, until the more successful officers reach the small group of those in highest authority.

As the careers of naval officers gradually progress, there is of necessity decrease in the number of officers in each of the ranks due to death, resignation, or retirement for physical disability. This decrease is not sufficient to insure adequate promotion, for it does not reduce the allowed number in each rank sufficiently to enable promotions to be made to bring officers to the successive ranks at an early enough age.

Unless some other method than seniority alone in promotion is used by the Navy, there would be stagnation in promotion, which would strike a mortal blow at the morale of the Navy.

The young officers are, as it were, pressing forward, and a steady flow of promotion for them must be found. This has been accomplished to a degree by selection in grade.

The distribution of officers in the various grades is fixed by law as a percentage of the whole. The percentages by the law are as follows:—

Rear Admiral	1%
Captain	4%
Commander	8%
Lieutenant Commander	15%
Lieutenant	30%
Lieutenant (J.G.) and Ensign	42%

After four years in a grade, an officer becomes eligible for promotion to the next higher grade. When selected, an officer's name is placed on a list, and he becomes eligible to promotion when a vacancy occurs and if he has had two years' sea service in his grade.

A certain flow of promotion thus follows in all ranks. The selection is made by boards appointed by the Navy Department. These boards of nine officers study the complete service record of all officers under consideration. A vote of six out of nine on the board is needed to select an officer.

The great problem in the system of selection is what to do with officers who are not selected, for they cannot be left in their active rank and see juniors pass over them. That would undermine any man's morale. Many of those who fail of selection are efficient, but lack of vacancies causes their elimination from active duty to the retired list when reaching a stipulated age.

These officers, after retirement, are not lost to the Naval Service. Their training, experience, and years of service make them a group of considerable value in an emergency. Every one of these officers who is physically capable would be called back on mobilization. They are thus a valuable reserve.

By the present system of selection the age of entering the various ranks in 1937 was calculated to be as follows:

Ensign	at 22	years
Lieutenant (J.G.)	" 25	"
Lieutenant	" 29	"
Lieutenant Commander .	" 36	"
Commander	" 43	"

Captain .... at 50 years
Rear Admiral .... " 56 "

Large increases in Navy personnel recently have lowered the ages somewhat.

Of the hundreds of midshipmen graduating annually at the Naval Academy, relatively few can expect to reach the grade of Rear Admiral, or even that of Captain. In a selection system, that result is only to be expected. Each officer must face a selection board at every rung of the ladder of advancement. Selection boards are not infallible; they sometimes make mistakes and promote officers who may not be as well fitted as others who are not selected. But in the aggregate, the best men will rarely be passed over, and those selected will be, if not the best, at least among the best fitted for advancement, and capable in training our fleet in peace and leading it in war.

Up to this point—since the primary function of the Naval Academy is to graduate future officers of the Line, officers who fight the ships—we have discussed only the procedure of promotion that applies to them. In the modern navy, however, there are several other types of officers whose positions you should understand.

In the early days, when warships were under sail, they were manned by both soldiers and sailors—the soldiers did the fighting, the sailors maneuvered the ships. Later, warships were manned by sailors and a few marines. The naval officers who sailed and fought the ships came to be called line officers. They belonged to the executive branch. All other officers on board were called staff officers and were ineligible to command, except in their own special departments.

Today line officers are those who perform executive duties, such as Captains of ships and officers who perform the duties of executive officer, navigator, gunnery officer, turret and gun division officer, watch officer, etc. These officers are trained to command men and to navigate and fight the ships. The line officer wears a gold star on his sleeve above the stripes indicating his rank.

Medical officers, naval constructors, supply officers and civil engineers, are staff officers and wear on their sleeve the emblem of their corps instead of the star of the line.

On board ship, and on the "Navy List," there is no distinction made between officers of the line and officers performing engineering duties. Yet many officers must be trained to specialize in engineering activities, more especially in designing. Each year a selected group of younger line officers are ordered to postgraduate work at leading engineering schools throughout the country.

Later in their careers certain of these officers may, upon their own request, be designated for engineering duty only. They remain on the "List" as line officers, but cannot be ordered to positions afloat to perform line duties.

The Naval Construction Corps of the Navy is composed of officers who have graduated from the Naval Academy and then, because of their special aptitude, have been selected to take postgraduate work at the Postgraduate School, and at leading technical schools to fit them to be naval architects. These officers cease to be line officers and are commissioned as junior lieutenants in the Construction Corps of the Navy.

The officers of the Civil Engineer Corps of the Navy

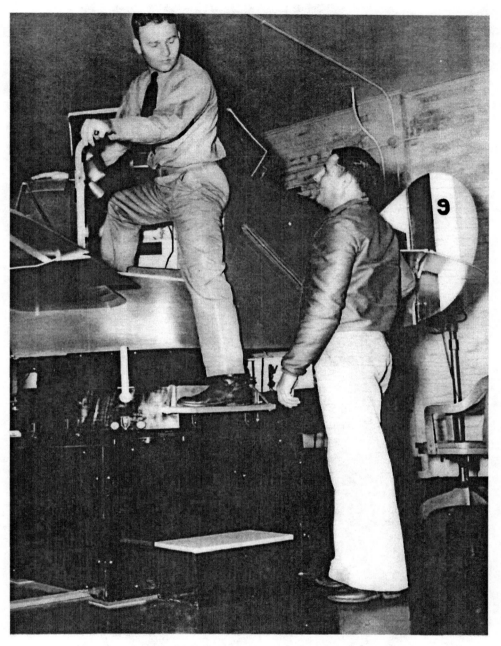

A student entering the Link Trainer, a model plane in which he learns all the intricacies of instrument flying. By the time he makes his first solo flight he is thoroughly at home with all the complicated instruments needed to judge altitude, speed, and to fly blind through rain or fog.

"Ground school" at Pensacola. A class studying the principles of aerial navigation which a young flier must know before he begins his instruction in the air.

Training planes on line at Corry Field, Pensacola.

A formation of advanced training planes above the clouds.

Advanced training planes on line at Corry Field.

Students beaching a patrol plane used for training.

A squadron of Scout-Bombers (SB2U-2) high above the clouds.

A section of Consolidated Patrol Planes, used by the Navy for long distance scouting and patrol duty.

A section of medium range Scout-Bombers (SB₂U-₁).

A section of Douglas Torpedo Bombers (TBD-1).

Close cooperation between aircraft and surface ships is essential. Here, during fleet maneuvers off California, planes are accompanying a line of battleships headed by a destroyer.

are, in the majority, graduates of the Naval Academy who have been given postgraduate work in civil engineering at technical institutes and then have been commissioned in that corps. Officers are occasionally admitted to this corps from civil life. They must be graduates of recognized technical schools and have had at least two years' practical experience as civil engineers. They must pass rigid mental and physical examinations before being commissioned as junior lieutenants in the corps.

Officers for the Supply Corps of the Navy are obtained from two sources: those who transfer from the regular line of the Navy subsequent to graduation from the Naval Academy, and those who enter the corps from civil life. The latter must be college graduates who have completed the Reserve Officers Training Corps course at one of the universities having units. All officers upon being taken into the Supply Corps are given a nine months' course at the Naval Finance and Supply School, located at Philadelphia.

Each year about 50 medical officers and from ten to fifteen dental officers are taken into the Navy as junior lieutenants. Applicants for these commissions must be graduates of medical schools rated "A" by the American Medical Association. They must pass a rigid physical examination before being eligible to take the competitive mental examination. Those who pass successfully are placed on a list in order of the mark received, and enter the service in the order of priority on this list.

Naturally enough, newly commissioned medical officers know little or nothing about the Navy they are entering, or of medical science as applied to the Navy. The Navy therefore maintains a medical school and dental school to acquaint these young men with the Naval Service, and the conditions under which they will work. New medical officers are ordered to these schools for an eight months' course. There they study the Navy Regulations and learn something of life on board ship and of the equipment they may expect to find there. At the same time they take up tropical medicine and receive short periods of instruction at the Marine Corps Base at Quantico, Virginia, and in field work at the Chemical Warfare School, Edgewood, Maryland, and in the study of poisonous gases.

CHAPTER IX

FROM THE FLEET TO SUBMARINE AND AIRPLANE DUTY

IT HAS been explained how the young ensign goes directly to a surface warship from the Naval Academy without further training and how, if he still stays in the line, he can expect to progress.

It has also been explained that after two years of service afloat he may request to be transferred to either the submarine or airplane branch of the fleet for further preparation. When we realize that the submarine and the airplane navigate in three dimensions instead of only two, we can understand the need of an expertness which can be obtained only through specialized training in these types of craft.

If the officer asks for submarine duty, and is accepted, he will go to the Submarine Base and School at New London, Connecticut, for a six months' course of study, followed by active service in submarines of the fleet—a branch of the service that is extremely popular with young officers because of the added excitement of serving underwater, because they attain positions of responsibility at an earlier age, and because the hazardous duty entitles them to higher pay.

At New London the students are given a course of study in all the instruments, machinery, and material that are contained within a submarine. The course of study includes the following subjects: (1) Submarine hull construction; (2) submarine motive power, Diesel engines and lead-acid storage batteries; (3) torpedo tubes and torpedoes; (4) system of flooding and blowing ballast tanks; (5) methods of trimming vessels to insure stability submerged; (6) optical studies, especially construction of periscopes.

Together with these theoretical and practical studies, the students obtain practice submerging a submarine. This practice is continued until the officer is expert.

The strategical and tactical uses of the submarine are studied, and officers must demonstrate their competence in making an attack on a target.

The school possesses what is called a diving tower, where the student is trained to use the escape lung from a depth of 100 feet, at a water pressure of nearly fifty pounds. This training is given to insure his expertness should a casualty require him to leave a submarine helpless on the bottom at a depth not too great for the use of the escape lung—approximately 300 feet.

After the student has successfully completed this submarine course, he is given a diploma and the submarine insignia, a pin which is a miniature gold submarine; this, like the wings of an aviator, is worn on the uniform, at the left breast. The officer then is available for duty in a submarine.

If, instead of choosing submarine duty, the officer asks for aviation duty—and is accepted—he goes to the aviation school at Pensacola, Florida. The thorough course he will take there to prepare himself as a naval aviation officer has been well described in a book of this series, *How to Be an Aviator* by Dick Merrill and George Daws.

The aviation course at Pensacola might be said to be

only a preliminary for actual aviation work in the fleet. The course gives personal expertness in flying and in all manner of maneuvers required both singly and in formation, but cannot give sufficient time to teach all the many things that will be needed to be known in actual flying in the fleet. That part will come gradually when the naval aviator goes on board a carrier, where he will be assigned to a plane in one of the airplane squadrons, operated from the ship.

The aircraft carrier is the Navy's mobile flying field. These carriers are massive ships of high speed capable of carrying and maintaining from sixty to eighty airplanes of different types. They are commanded, and in large part manned, by officers who have had aviation training, many of them qualified aviators. These vessels are organized into a squadron now consisting of six ships and commanded by an Admiral. The squadron is an important adjunct of the fleet and is proving to be a unit that must always be present with the fleet. A fleet today without an adequate air force in carriers is almost as defenseless as a fleet without guns.

The aircraft carrier is a very vulnerable vessel and must be carefully guarded and protected when at sea. It carries some guns, 8-inch and 6-inch in caliber, but these would not be sufficient to safeguard it against a fast battleship or cruiser with more and heavier gun power.

On such a carrier, the aviator who has completed the course at Pensacola will obtain wide experience in formation flying and in navigation, in all kinds of weather, fair and foul, and even in fogs. He must become expert in flying off and on the carrier under good conditions and also under conditions of weather none too safe, but in which the Admiral or Captain of the air squadron may decide it is necessary to operate the planes. Systematic training will be given him in practice bombing, fighting, scouting, spotting the fall of salvos, and so on. His training will be progressive and he will soon feel comfortably at home in his work.

Here the two or more years he has already served in surface warships of the fleet—usually one year at least in a battleship and then an additional year in a destroyer—will stand him in good stead and prove the wisdom of the Bureau of Navigation's policy.

The Navy knows that an aviator is more useful after he has become familiar with the fleet work in surface ships. An aviator who cannot identify at a glance the type of warship from the air, or fails to recognize his own ships, distinguishing them from ships of an enemy, is useless to the Navy, even though he may be an excellent aviator, until he can acquire this important knowledge.

Who does not know of the historical flight of the famed NC 4, a Navy patrol plane that succeeded in flying to Europe from America via the Azores in 1919? The NC 4 was flown by Lieutenant A. C. Read, a naval aviator. It was a marvelous achievement at that time and Lieutenant Read won the plaudits of the world. He is now a Captain in the Navy, commanding the Navy Air Station at Pensacola.

In preparing this book, I wrote him inquiring about the present course for aviators and received the response given below. I am publishing his letter, not only because it contains information in regard to the training being given to civilians to qualify them to fly the naval planes,

but also because I am sure it will be most stimulating
to our young naval officer aspirants to read a letter
from Captain Read, and to know that such a well-known
and accomplished naval aviation expert is in charge of the
course of training for the aviators of the Navy. The letter
might be considered an open letter to the prospective
young naval aviators of America. I quote from Captain
Read's letter:

"Upon selection for training, the student is sent to the
Naval Reserve Air Base nearest to his home or resi-
dence. There are thirteen such bases located strategically
throughout the country. The student spends one month
at the Reserve Base during which time he receives ten
hours instruction in primary flying and approximately
one hour solo. In keeping with this phase of his training
he receives indoctrination in such subjects as navigation,
radio transmission and reception, military drill, manual
of arms, seamanship and any other general information
as the time allows.

"During this time, which is classified as elimination
training, the student is enrolled as a seaman second class
and receives the corresponding rate of pay plus flight
pay, or $54, and his uniforms and subsistence.

"If a student meets all the requirements of elimination
training satisfactorily he is then sent to Pensacola to further his career. He is now classed as an aviation cadet
and receives $75 per month, plus subsistence, $1 per
diem, and uniforms.

"The present syllabus is for a period of seven months
and covers all phases of flying from primary to advanced
work. Subjects in the flight syllabus include aerial stunts,

precision work, formation, cross-country, patrol work, combat, gunnery, instrument flying, and catapults.

"The student's day begins early and never lags. Reveille is at 0500, flying begins at 0700 and continues until 1600. (5.00 A.M., 7.00 A.M., and 4.00 P.M.) The students attend Ground School one half of the day and fly in the various squadrons during the other half. They are free until dinner after which they attend more ground school classes, if deficient, or spend their time leisurely as the case may be.

"Training is closely supervised and constantly improved. The student receives close medical supervision and care. His social life is on the same plane as that of the officers.

"Regular naval officers, upon selection, come to Pensacola directly from the fleet and receive a very similar training. The Navy also trains a number of enlisted personnel each year and those who complete the course are known as aviation pilots."

A bow view of the aircraft carrier USS Saratoga with her complement of planes ready for the take-off. This floating landing field carries seventy-nine planes, including fighters, scouts, and torpedo bombers. Of its 1,899 officers and men (including flying personnel), 169 are commissioned officers. Originally authorized in 1916 as a battle cruiser, the Saratoga was altered when the war demonstrated the need for such carriers. The flight deck is 880 feet long, about 85 feet wide, and 60 feet above the water line.

Four of the five aircraft carriers now in commission photographed together: USS *Lexington*, USS *Ranger*, USS *Yorktown*, and USS *Enterprise*, carrying a total of more than 350 aircraft and almost 8,000 officers and men. They travel at an average speed of better than 30 knots.

A surface view of the massive aircraft carrier USS *Yorktown*.

Heavy cruisers accompanied by aircraft during fleet maneuvers. In an actual engagement, these planes would protect the surface ships from attack, serve as scouts and observers.

Aerial view of the aircraft carrier USS *Enterprise* taken while her more than 100 planes were all aloft. The planes take off from, and land on, the deck, which is identified on either end for the pilots by the first two letters of the ship's name. Commissioned in 1936, the ship carries 2,072 officers and men, including the flying personnel.

A left Eschelon formation of Grumman fighter planes (F2F-1) used for
attack and to protect bombers.

The destroyer USS *Farragut*. Slightly heavier than the others in its class, it
weighs 1,395 tons and has a radius of 6,000 miles. It carries 162 officers and
men, is armed with five 5-inch guns, four machine guns, and eight 21-inch
torpedo tubes.

CHAPTER X

FROM ENSIGN TO DEVIL DOG

Each year, instead of going directly into the fleet and then perhaps into the submarine or airplane branches, approximately twenty-five Naval Academy graduates go directly from Annapolis to the United States Marine Corps as second lieutenants. These account for the majority of Marine Corps officers. The others are appointed in various ways; five are appointed from within the ranks of the Corps, the remainder from either officers of the Marine Corps Reserve or from honor graduates of selected colleges and universities who have had advanced training with units of the Army or Navy Reserve Officers Training Corps—the ROTC.

The Marine Corps is a colorful, two-fisted branch of the service, justly celebrated in popular fiction. In wartime it fights a swift, close action. It might almost be called the hinge between land and sea. When the Navy has secured an advantage, opened up a harbor, it is then the Marine Corps' job to nail that advantage to the shore. Assisted by the pounding of the big Navy guns, it prepares the way for the landing of troops. If this country is ever attacked and if any force attempts to touch our soil, it will find the Marine Corps bristling on the beach.

The Marine Corps came into being in 1775, when the first Congress passed a resolution organizing two Marine Corps battalions. In those days—the days of sailing ships—these marines fought the ship's guns, boarded the adversary, or repelled boarders. They were armed with muskets and kept up a continuous fire upon the enemy exposed to their view.

Kipling called the marine, "soldier and sailor too." He is today a soldier of the sea.

During the Revolutionary War marines in small detachments served in all warships, and performed heroic service. At the conclusion of the war the corps was disbanded but was reorganized in 1798 to participate in the undeclared war with France in that year.

In the War of 1812 the Marines fought in nearly every engagement ashore or afloat, including those of the historic *Constitution*, and the battles of Lake Erie and Lake Champlain.

In the War between the States, the Marine Corps served in the blockading ships of the Navy and participated in naval attacks on the coastal fortifications of the Confederacy.

In the Spanish War a Marine company was stationed in each of the larger ships of the Navy. A large force of marines landed under the guns of the Navy at Guantanamo Bay, Cuba, and after severe fighting with the enemy helped to secure the harbor as a base for Admiral W. T. Sampson's fleet blockading Admiral Cevera's fleet in Santiago harbor.

While a component part of the Naval Service, marines may be detached for service with the Army as they were in France during the first World War.

Marines have taken part when naval ships have been ordered to land armed men in countries of the American Continent where revolutions were jeopardizing the lives and property of American citizens, in order to protect American interests.

During the Marine Corps' existence its greatest strength was 75,000, during the World War. The strength recommended today is 20 per cent of the personnel of the Navy. This number would today give the Corps about 25,000 men, and would fulfill peacetime requirements and maintain units in readiness to support the fleet in case of war.

The Marine Corps is under the command of a Major General Commandant. The Corps might be said to have four distinct tasks in support of the Navy, as follows:

1. To maintain a mobile force in readiness as a part of the fleet for use in operations involving shore objectives.

2. To maintain marine detachments in battleships, cruisers, and aircraft carriers.

3. To provide guards for safeguarding of navy yards and naval stations at home and in our outlying possessions.

4. To provide forces for the protection of American lives and property abroad.

There is organized, as an integral part of the fleet, a marine force of all arms known as the Fleet Marine Force. This organization is based on shore but for a period of two months each year it takes part in landing exercises with units of the fleet. It is composed of infantry, artillery (including antiaircraft guns), aviation, tanks, signal troops, engines, and chemical troops.

Ensigns graduating from the Naval Academy who ask for service with the Marine Corps, and are accepted as second lieutenants, attend the Basic School at the Navy Yard, Philadelphia, for a course of one year in the duties of a lieutenant of marines at sea, in the field or in garrison. Later in their career they go to the Marine Corps School in Quantico, Virginia, where they are given more advanced instructions.

For higher military training, marine officers are sent to the Naval War College, the Army War College, Army Command General Staff School, Infantry School, Signal Corps School, Coast Artillery School, Army Air Service Tactical and Technical Schools.

The ranks of officers in the marines correspond to those of the Army, and their pay is similar to the pay of the Army and Navy of relative rank and length of service.

The Marine Corps Reserve consists of two classes: the Fleet Reserve and the Volunteer Reserve. The Fleet Reserve is required to drill once weekly and to attend fifteen days' annual training. There are now eighteen infantry battalions, one artillery battalion, and ten aviation squadrons stationed in various cities of the country. These organizations are fully equipped with military accoutrements for their branch of the service. The Volunteer Reserve is grouped into reserve regiments for administrative purposes only, and is not required to attend weekly drills or annual field training.

The selection of young qualified Reserve Officers is made from college students in their sophomore year. They are enlisted in the Volunteer Reserve and are assigned to two weeks' intensive training during the summer vacation at the end of the sophomore and junior years in college. After successfully completing the two periods of training and upon graduation from college, the young men are commissioned as second lieutenants in the Marine Corps Reserve.

College graduates are accepted as aviation cadets in the Marine Corps Reserve and receive flight training and instruction at the Naval Air Station, Pensacola, Florida. The young men who successfully complete this course receive three years of flight training with Marine Corps squadrons, and then are commissioned first lieutenants in the Reserve. After receiving their commissions, promotion is dependent upon an officer's interest, activity, and ability.

At this writing two forces of United States Marines are maintained in China: at Peiping a Marine detachment acts as legation guard; and there is a regiment of marines at Shanghai.

A squadron of Marine airplanes is based at St. Thomas in the Virgin Islands. This unit is on detached duty from the Fleet Marine Force and is operating directly under the headquarters of the Marine Corps.

The work of the Marine Corps is varied and interesting. Morale is high, and the life of a Marine officer is an occupation and an adventure well worth the hard work necessary to become one.

CHAPTER XI

NAVAL RESERVE AND COAST GUARD

WE HAVE assumed up to this point that the young man who wants to be a naval officer makes his decision before he has finished high school, or even earlier. In which case he tries for an appointment to the Naval Academy.

There are still several entrances into the Navy for young men who decide on a naval career later in life, while they are in college or after they have been graduated. To these young men there are opportunities to become officers in either the Naval Reserve or the Coast Guard.

The reason for the Naval Reserve is this: In the event of a war with a first class power, our Navy will require many more officers than are now allowed to be commissioned in the regular Navy—these officers must come from sources other than the Naval Academy. The Naval Reserve consists of three classes: The Fleet Naval Reserve, The Merchant Marine Naval Reserve, and The Volunteer Naval Reserve. It is composed of male citizens of the United States and its insular possessions 17 years of age or over, who by appointment therein obligate themselves to serve in the Navy in time of war or during the existence of national emergency.

The Fleet Naval Reserve is most intimately associated with the regular Navy. Its members hold weekly drills and make annual cruises on naval vessels.

The Merchant Marine Naval Reserve is composed of licensed officers of the American Merchant Marine who are serving on vessels approved by the Navy Department.

The Volunteer Naval Reserve is composed of those who are not able to devote the time required of the Fleet Naval Reserve, and include individuals whose capabilities fit them for such service as naval constructors, civil engineers, medical officers, etc.

In addition to the Naval Reserve, a valuable source of officer material is turned out annually by the Reserve Officers Training Corps units maintained in leading universities throughout the country.

Any young man who has graduated from college, especially with a scientific degree, and who is physically perfect, might well aspire to become a naval reserve officer. In time of emergency the Naval Reserve goes through a rapid expansion, and capable, well-educated young men are needed by Uncle Sam for his Navy. If a person has made up his mind to serve in the Navy as an officer, let him present himself at the nearest Naval Headquarters where he will find out what he must do to be able to take the examination required.

Recently, in line with our Government's policy of rapid expansion of all military branches, still further provision has been made for the training of naval reserve officers. Under this program, five thousand young men are being given an intensive course of practical and theoretical study which, when completed, will give them the rank of Naval Reserve Ensigns. The requirements are set forth as follows in a recent issue of the *U. S. Naval Institute Proceedings*:

Five thousand young men having a minimum of two years of college education are to be enlisted in the naval reserve in a new class designated as V-7 and given one month of training at sea under a routine similar to that used for naval ROTC students for many years past. The Government will pay the railway fare and subsistence of successful applicants en route to and from their homes. The students will receive no pay, but will be given their food, lodging, uniforms, books, and equipment, so that no direct expense will be involved for those accepted. Upon completion of this training cruise of one month, which will be conducted on a competitive basis, selected candidates will be eligible for appointment by the Secretary of the Navy as naval reserve midshipmen. Naval reserve midshipmen will then be eligible to take a further course of three months' special instruction on shore, leading to qualification for commissions as ensigns in the volunteer reserve for general line duties. Naval reserve midshipmen while undergoing the three months' course of instruction will receive the same pay and allowances as midshipmen of the regular Navy. The three months' special course as a naval reserve midshipman may be deferred at the request of the individual so as not to interfere with his college courses or other civilian activities.

The Navy Department intends to make available three battleships in the Atlantic, the first cruise to commence about July 16 on the *Wyoming*. These cruises will continue until about January 15, 1941. The embryo officers will be given intensive training in gunnery, navigation, engineering, communications, and watchstanding at sea. The first 90-day course for naval reserve midshipmen will be conducted in the U.S.S. *Illinois* at New York commencing upon the completion of the first cruise of the *Wyoming* on or about August 17. These instruction periods on the *Illinois* will continue as long as necessary.

Should the number of applicants for the 90-day instruction exceed the capacity of the *Illinois*, arrangements for such instruction in the Chicago area will be provided. Further expansion of this phase, if necessary, will be provided for,

Marines of the Fleet Marine Force operating a trench mortar, a weapon of increasing importance in recent years, and just one of the many weapons which make the Marines all-around fighting men.

Marines on duty in Shanghai guarding a machine gun nest covering the approach to the International Settlement. Because of Sino-Japanese troubles, Marines in the Orient have been constantly on the alert in recent years.

A Marine officer instructs newly-recruited sea soldiers in the important art of adjusting the rifle sling, a detail essential to good marksmanship.

A signal outfit of the Marine Corps stationed in Shanghai establishing a telephone exchange on an abandoned incense burner near a Lama temple. This is just part of the job of guarding lives and property of United States citizens in time of stress.

Marines during practice maneuvers in the West Indies. They are crouching low in a motor-sailing launch to avoid the simulated gun-fire of an enemy attempting to keep them from landing on the beach.

Marines have a sense of humor, as demonstrated by the names given to these big 155-mm guns, "Mae West," "Popeye," "Big Bad Wolf," and "Tarzan." Marines pride themselves on their expert knowledge of all weapons, from these monsters down to automatic pistols.

Marines at their base in San Diego display their equipment on the grass in front of their barracks, one of the finest buildings of its kind in the country.

A pack howitzer is readied for action by a group of Marines at the Marine Corps Base at Quantico, Virginia.

A motorized unit of Marines drives through the street of Peiping, China, where for more than thirty years detachments of Marines have guarded the American Legation of the American Embassy.

The Fleet Marine Corps assembled for a parade at San Diego, one of the principal bases of the United States Navy and the Marine Corps.

Detachments of Marines serve aboard all first class battleships and cruisers. Here the Marines aboard the USS *Indianapolis* present arms for an inspection by the ship's captain.

Constant drill keeps the Marine ready for action at any time. Here members of the Marine Corps Expeditionary Force at Shanghai, China, are engaged in range-finding and target spotting drill.

A Marine student being instructed in the care and repair of small arms at the Armorers School in Philadelphia. He is developed a skill highly important to the functioning of any modern military establishment.

Off to the Orient! A detachment of Marines embarking from San Diego for service in China. The Marines are the amphibians of the military service, readily adapting themselves to duty ashore or afloat.

An anti-aircraft battery of 50-caliber machine guns engaging in practice at Quantico, Virginia, one of the mobilization points from which Marines frequently leave for maneuvers in the Caribbean.

first in the California area and then in the New Orleans area. Facilities will also be available for this instruction at the Naval Academy for one class of approximately 500 naval reserve midshipmen beginning in February, 1941.

Naval reserve midshipmen who successfully complete the 90-day course will be given commissions as ensigns in the volunteer naval reserve for general line duties. If present world conditions continue there will be opportunity for many naval reserve ensigns to serve on active duty in the fleet with full pay and allowances.

Candidates to be acceptable must present birth certificates to prove they are American-born and be between 19 and 26 years of age, unmarried. They must present abstracts of their college records showing that they have completed successfully not less than two years of college at accredited institutions and have written recommendations from at least two responsible citizens. Candidates under 21 years of age must have the signed consent of their legal guardian. The physical requirements for acceptance will be the same as for Naval Academy graduates who are commissioned in the regular Navy.

Applicants may apply at the headquarters of the naval district or the naval reserve unit or navy recruiting station nearest their homes, where application forms will be made out and physical examinations conducted.

Another valuable reinforcement to the Navy in war time is our own efficient Coast Guard Service. It is, in fact, a miniature Navy, with its own Naval School at New London, Conn., for the education and training of its officers. The Coast Guard Service is under the Treasury Department in time of peace, but in war automatically becomes an integral part of the Navy, and is then administered by the Navy Department.

The Coast Guard vessels are designed to fit into the Navy's requirements in time of war. There are a number of Coast Guard cutters of about 2,000 tons and over 20 knots speed, especially valuable to fight the submarine. The Coast Guard also has an air corps and a personnel of accomplished fliers.

The work of the Coast Guard in all kinds of weather, going to the rescue of ships in distress off our coast, has made the personnel develop into hardy and resourceful seamen, most welcome to the Navy in war. The Coast Guard carry out a routine on board their ships similar to that of the Navy, even to gunnery training and target practice with guns up to 5-inch in caliber.

CHAPTER XII

SAILING ASHORE

WHEN the average civilian hears the word "Navy," he naturally thinks of warships, of the big guns he has seen pointing their muzzles at him in the newsreels, or of rows of seamen standing at attention on a breezy deck. Of course this is all a part of the Navy—and the really vital part—but the naval ships for fighting on the seas, which in the aggregate are called the fleet, would soon find themselves derelicts if it weren't for a great organization that stands behind the fleet to administer to its needs. This organization is the Navy Department.

Any young man considering a career in the Navy should thoroughly understand the Navy Department and its many important functions. There are thousands of vital jobs to be done there by men who in some cases never go to sea but who are none the less naval men.

The justification for the vast Navy Department is evident to any student of naval history, which shows how often the administration of naval affairs has been the deciding factor in victory or defeat. Ships and men are vital, of course, but efficient administration must be behind them before you can have what is known as "Sea Power." It is Sea Power that wins wars. Our Navy owes its existence to our Country's recognition of the need of sea power for the nation. The neglect of sea power by nations that can be reached by sea has always proved disastrous. The reason is evident. The sea is a natural military road leading direct to the shores of those countries whose borders touch the ocean. It is a road that cannot be destroyed. The one way to block it against an enemy is by the acquisition of sea power sufficient to make an attempted invasion from overseas so hazardous as to be an unprofitable venture for even the strongest sea power.

The fate of North America was determined by sea power. If British sea power had not been superior to that of France, the larger part of North America would not have been a British colony, but a French one.

In the American Revolution, the Americans won their independence through the aid of French sea power. A fleet under the French Admiral, Count De Grasse, fought the British fleet under Admiral Graves in a naval action off the Capes of the Chesapeake, and although the action was not decisive, the result was to permit Admiral De Grasse's ships, with reenforcements and war material being furnished by France to General Washington at Yorktown, to reach its destination, thus compelling the surrender of General Cornwallis' army to General Washington. This surrender culminated in the granting of American independence from England. We now know that Admiral De Grasse, more than any other man except Washington himself, made American independence possible.

Napoleon was overthrown by the sea power of England.

The sea power of the Northern States preserved the Union in the War between the States by cutting off trade with neutrals, and slowly throttling the Confederacy.

In the first World War, the Allies won in the end because of their superior sea power.

Upon the efficiency of our naval administration today, the safety of our country and the lives of our citizens will depend.

The fundamental naval policy of the United States is to maintain the Navy in sufficient strength to support the national policies and our commerce, and to guard the continental and overseas possessions of our country.

The President of the United States is the Commander-in-Chief of the entire naval establishment, and administers this vast organization through the Secretary of the Navy, a civilian, who is an officer in his cabinet.

Under the Secretary is the General Board, consisting of the highest ranking naval officers, chosen by the Secretary. The General Board is a purely consulting body, and exercises no authority.

The Chief of Naval Operations is a high ranking officer of the Navy, usually a Rear Admiral, appointed by the President. Under the Secretary of the Navy, the selected Chief of Naval Operations becomes the senior officer of the Navy, and is given the rank of Admiral. He is charged with the operations of the fleet and the preparation and readiness of plans for its use in war. His detailed duties will be found in the appendix.

One of his important duties is the supervision of the naval districts into which the United States has been divided for the administration of the complex yet essential naval shore establishment. Each of these districts is under the command of a Rear Admiral. Formerly there were sixteen of these districts. Now Puerto Rico has been added.

The largest of the Navy's shore activities are navy yards. Navy yards are located where naval ships can be built, drydocked, repaired, and extensive alterations effected. A naval station is a place where ships can be supplied with fuel, ammunition, necessary stores and effect minor repairs. Besides the navy yards, the Navy maintains a large number of other shore establishments for the purpose of serving the fleet. The Bureau of Ordnance administers several shore establishments engaged in the production of material and weapons furnished the Navy by that Bureau. They include gun factories, powder factories, proving grounds, torpedo stations, mine depots —every sort of establishment, in fact, that is necessary to provide the Navy with modern weapons. All in all, it is an immense organization devoted to the storage, overhauling, and assembly of ammunition. In the ammunition depots alone, some 15,000 civilians are employed. About 800 civilians are employed in the various shore establishments maintained by the Bureau of Engineering, including research laboratories and experimental stations for testing materials.

There are also bureaus devoted variously to Aeronautics (nine airplane establishments are maintained), Construction and Repair, Yards and Docks, Engineering, Supplies and Accounts, and Medicine and Surgery.

In addition, there are some seven or eight boards largely devoted to the important tasks of coördination.

As you can see, the organization of the Navy is a wide and wonderful thing. A closer study of the appendix will give you the exact function and location of all its establishments as well as the functions of the boards. Little seems to have been omitted. I cannot refrain from saying, however, that there is one body lacking, which should be the crown piece of the structure: That would be a Navy General Staff, composed of officers who are free from all administrative duties and who study and plan for every step in the progress of making our Navy the best fighting machine on the seas.

CHAPTER XIII

THE NAVY'S FAMILY TREE

BY THIS time you should have a fairly complete picture of our Navy today—of the way its officers are trained and of the vast, unseen machinery that keeps it going. For a complete understanding of the Navy, however, you need to know something of how navies were evolved and for what they were created.

We know that ships sailed the seas carrying merchandise before the idea of warships ever was conceived. Trade rivalry between citizens of different nations caused friction which soon was translated into acts of violence against peaceful ships, their merchandise and their crews. To defend their merchant ships, nations then placed soldiers on board them, and when that did not offer security enough, separate ships were supplied carrying soldiers to fight similar ships of rivals. These latter ships were afterward called warships.

Soldiers fought on land many centuries before they fought at sea. In the fighting on land, military men discovered principles of land warfare which naturally were applicable to fighting on the seas.

On land, numbers usually had brought victory, hence the obvious thing was to build warships capable of carrying more and more soldiers, and with ample deck space for these soldiers to wield their weapons.

On land, victory also depended upon the speedy transportation of soldiers in overwhelming numbers to

The Marine Radio School at San Diego gives the Marine a knowledge of radio and various other forms of signalling. Here he is prepared for duty in any of the signal units to which he may be assigned.

A smaller Coast Guard cutter, 165 feet long, one of the group built in 1934. Normally, they carry more than sixty officers and men and have a cruising radius of more than 5,000 miles.

One of the Coast Guard's modern lifeboats. These sturdy, motor-driven boats are a vital part of the equipment at more than 300 Coast Guard units.

A Coast Guard cabin picket boat, 38 feet long. Speedy and flexible, these vessels are often called upon when the use of larger craft is impracticable.

A 165-foot Coast Guard patrol boat, one of the many valuable steel vessels in constant service along the nation's coastline to protect commercial shipping and pleasure craft. They stand ready to assist the Navy in any major crisis.

A Grumman sea-plane—one of the various types of flying boat in Coast Guard service. They are valuable in peacetime patrol duty and invaluable in time of war.

A Coast Guard cutter with a disabled trawler in tow. One of the major
duties of the Coast Guard is giving assistance to disabled vessels. During the
fiscal year of 1939 the Coast Guard rescued more than 10,000 persons
from tight spots.

The International Ice Patrol maintained by the Coast Guard keeps close tab
on such dangerous icebergs as this, warning vessels of their position and course.
Since the formation of the Patrol shortly after the sinking of the *Titanic*,
there has not been a single disaster caused by collision with a berg.

a crucial point for attack or defense. Therefore ships were built for speed and to outmaneuver the enemy's ships.

The propulsion of ships first was with oars, in the days of the galleons. To gain greater speed, extra tiers of oarsmen were provided. The ships ran alongside their enemy and the soldiers fought hand to hand. This method of fighting continued until the power of cannon made that method too costly to life.

Sail power followed oar power. The great three-deckers of the eighteenth century were floating fortresses, but because of their bulk were comparatively slow even under great press of canvas. They fought their antagonists yardarm to yardarm, the object being to fire their large number of guns at point-blank range and then to carry the enemy ship with a boarding party. In such close actions, with gun muzzles actually touching, it was believed that gun power could not decide an action on the sea. Boarding was employed to achieve capture and victory. Guns only prepared the way for the final assault. But when the range of cannon increased, warships then fought with clear water between them. Destruction by gunfire, rather than by boarding, then became the means to victory.

Against the destructive effect of gunfire, even in the days of wooden ships, the heavily timbered sides of ships offered some protection from cannon balls. Later anchor chains were hung along the ship's sides and lashed. And lastly, armor was bolted to the wooden sides. The size of warships gradually increased to give great gun power, speed, and protection against the enemy's fire.

Sail gave place to steam propulsion. Wood gave place to iron, then to steel.

The warship owes its conception and evolution to the urgent need for soldiers to fight on the sea. Today this fighting is performed with long-range cannon, torpedoes, and airplane bombs.

The great line of battleships of the days of Admiral Nelson, in fighting on the seas, represented the infantry and artillery in fighting on land. The use of cavalry on land for the purpose of scouting and reconnaissance—when applied to fighting on the sea—prompted the design of a warship to perform a similar purpose. The frigate was the result. When the line of battleships with their many tiers of cannon slowly grew to become in after years our dreadnaught battleship, the frigate changed its appearance entirely and became what we call today a cruiser.

The great fighting ship, the battleship, became the infantry and the artillery of the seas rolled into one. It continued to increase in size, and to multiply the number and caliber of its guns. Armor protection kept pace with the penetrating ability of the great shells fired by the guns.

Iron and steel ships followed the general lines of the wooden ships. Guns at first were placed in broadside. The American *Monitor* discarded the broadside arrangement and was a revolution in type. It was a new idea, embodying a new principle in shipbuilding: guns in turrets. From this type followed in due course the turret battleships. A long time elapsed between the original *Monitor* that fought the *Merrimac* and our newest dreadnaughts, the *Washington* and the *North Carolina* recently launched; it was three-quarters of a century, but the natural conservatism of the sea first had to be overcome.

Gun power and armor protection slowly developed in effectiveness, but greatly accelerated as the industrial arts increased in efficiency. Greater size of ships became necessary to carry the weight added in guns, armor, and ammunition. Length always has been a restricted dimension in warship construction because of the difficulties in stability; in consequence the width—or beam—and the depth of ships increased enormously, making the navigation of harbors more difficult, and necessitating the widening and deepening of our ports of entry. Today the width of the Panama Canal has placed a limit upon the beam of our great ships in order that they may safely navigate the Canal between the two oceans.

On March 4th, 1861, a month before hostilities opened in our Civil War, there were just twelve national vessels in service on the Atlantic Coast of the United States. The stern necessities of war increased this number by December 1 to 264 warships, carrying a total of 2,557 guns and 22,000 sailors. Half of these were built and half purchased. All were manned by untrained men and their cost was enormous. Over one-half were steamers, including three ironclads and twenty-three first-class gunboats. By 1865 the United States Navy was second to none. Its ships were battle-scarred veterans and the personnel had been trained throughout four long years of actual conflict. A new type of ironclad had been built and proved. The *Monitor* led in formidableness and effectiveness all other types of warships. Yet once the war was ended, Congress gave no further heed to the navy which had been the most potent instrument for success to the Union cause. The Navy was permitted to fall into dry rot. Ships were sold or "scrapped" and sailors discharged.

Finally the war with Spain embarked us upon the sea of Empire. It was not until then that our statesmen seemed suddenly to appreciate the value of naval force as a potential argument of diplomacy. Now that appreciation happily seems to be universal. The difficulty lies in determining the minimum strength of the naval force required in order that the argument may be won without the use of that force dynamically.

CHAPTER XIV

THE FLEET TODAY

ALL of these historical factors and many others have contributed to the development of the United States fleet as it stands today—the spearhead of our national defense and the guardian of the Nation's security against aggression.

For strategical and tactical purposes the fleet is now organized into major units: Battle Force, Scouting Force, Submarine Force, and Base Force. To facilitate administration, repair, and upkeep, these forces are organized into the categories of the several types of warships comprising them: battleships, cruisers, aircraft carriers and aircraft, destroyers, and submarines. Each of these is the result of evolution. All have a special function; no single type can be given all the offensive and defensive qualities that might be desired. To design a warship to fulfill its function, three factors are always taken into consideration: gun power, armor, and speed. To obtain greater gun power, a proportion of speed and armor must be sacrificed or the ship will be too heavy. In destroyers and cruisers, speed is considered the essential; in battleships, gun power and armor are emphasized.

The battleship has long been regarded as the embodiment of naval power. Its principal armament is guns in armored turrets; as many guns of the maximum caliber as possible are carried. At the present moment we have fifteen battleships in commission and eight being built to replace those that are over-age. These new ships are to have thirteen 16-inch guns. The two largest will weigh 45,000 tons and have a speed of about 30 knots.

The United States Navy never has built battle cruisers. The new battleships being built will be of higher speed than the older ships, and will have a greater number of guns and a thicker armor. A battle cruiser, theoretically, sacrifices some of its gun power and some thickness of armor to enable it to be given an increased speed. A battle cruiser therefore is of less fighting power than a battleship.

The cruisers of our Navy are limited to two types—heavy and light cruisers. The heavy cruisers carry 8-inch caliber guns, are of very high speed, and are 10,000 tons displacement. The light cruisers are of similar speed and tonnage, but carry 6-inch caliber guns. Cruisers are used for many important purposes; a most critical one is for the protection of commerce on the seas.

Destroyers today are used for very wide purposes; probably the one most frequently mentioned in the war is the fight with depth charges against the submarines.

In addition to the destroyer, other fast types of warships of small size such as the patrol vessel, the submarine chaser and the sloop, are used to combat the submarine. Submarines are armed either with torpedoes or mines, and often with both weapons. The principal weapons against them are depth charges dropped from surface warships, and bombs dropped by airplanes.

The above classes of vessels might be considered the fighting types of warships. In addition, to serve the fleet there are many auxiliary vessels. Some are of a mili-

tary character, while others are for the upkeep and
supply of warships. Those of a military character are
mine layers, mine sweepers and gunboats. The non-
military vessels are repair ships, ammunition ships, supply ships, fuel ships, tenders for destroyers and submarines, hospital ships, mine depot ships, net-laying
ships, tugs, and miscellaneous. All these types are required in correct proportion to serve the fleet.

The fleet must have naval bases from which to operate.
The auxiliaries mentioned might be said to constitute
a floating base which will require only a sheltered anchorage to make it useful. In important areas there must
be naval land bases, such as that at Pearl Harbor, Hawaii,
from which the fleet can operate in war.

We have learned that the United States is building
a number of naval bases both in the Atlantic Ocean and
in the Pacific. Such naval bases, if well and strategically
located, are vital to the success of a campaign on the
seas.

During the last two decades the perfection of two
new weapons of warfare—the submarine, with its torpedoes, the airplane, with its aerial bombs—have greatly
influenced not only naval tactics but the design of naval
craft. Their importance is being demonstrated now in
the present world conflict.

The invention of the airplane is responsible for the
airplane bomb. Today we know that the air weapon
is the most important menace to the prestige of the
battleship.

The torpedo has made subdivision of the warship's
hull necessary to localize damage to the bottom, and
the airplane bomb has made the ship designers increase

the thickness of steel decks to minimize bomb explosions. The invention of the torpedo is responsible for the creation of ships to carry these weapons: the torpedo boat and the destroyer. Later the invention of the submarine was achieved to carry these torpedo weapons. In our submarines we have arrived at a vessel of long radius of action and high surface speed. These qualities have necessitated a tonnage of about 1,500 tons. Essentially the submarine of this type is an offensive warship. It can carry the war across an ocean and can remain away from its base for months. It is armed with both torpedoes and guns. Some are also fitted to lay mines.

The mine is a weapon that has proved dangerous to all vessels at sea. They have done great damage in the present war, as they did in the last one. Defenses against them have been developed, of course. The contact mine has been rendered harmless by an invention called the paravane. Now the magnetic mine menace is being overcome by an electric cable wound around the outside of a ship, giving the vessel an electric field to prevent the mine from operating. Nevertheless, belligerents at war must constantly sweep waters where mines are suspected, such as entrances to harbors or narrow channels. Mine sweepers are used for this purpose—usually tugs of light draft with sweeps towed astern to cut the mine anchor cable and allow the mine to come to the surface where it can be exploded by gun fire.

One thing seems certain, if we can trust the historical records of weapons of war: A new and radical weapon at first succeeds because of the element of surprise; then, after a time, methods are found to render it less harmful. For instance, the penetration of the steel explosive

A cutter frees a tug and a barge held fast by ice in the Hudson River, just part of the constant service rendered by the Coast Guard in all kinds of weather.

The Coast Guard Patrol Boat *Pandora* leading the annual fishing trophy parade at Miami. Each year the Coast Guard patrols hundreds of such marine parades and regattas, supervising marine traffic, and standing by for any emergency.

A dramatic picture of the Coast Guard in action: Coast Guard seaplane arriving just in time to rescue the crew from a burning boat at sea.

Coast Guard activities are not confined to the high seas, as demonstrated by this picture of a motor-driven surfboat removing refugees from the flooded area around Paducah, Kentucky, during the great flood of 1937.

Military maneuvers and drills form a large part of the four-year course for future officers at the Coast Guard Academy at New London, Connecticut.

A number of training stations are maintained by the Coast Guard for licensed and unlicensed personnel of the Merchant Marine. Here members of the Maritime Service are receiving instruction in handling lines, splicing, etc. Other instruction is given in various branches of navigation and marine engineering.

Coast Guard station at Humboldt Bay, typical of the nearly 300 such that dot the nation's coastline, each with the most modern equipment necessary to give aid either near the station or at a distance.

One of the Coast Guard Air Stations maintained at many strategic points with trained pilots always on call. Planes have demonstrated their value in transporting sick or injured persons from ships at sea, in conveying storm warnings to vessels not equipped with radio, in flood relief work, and in the suppression of smuggling.

From sunset to sunrise members of the Coast Guard patrol our beaches as policemen patrol our streets, alert for any sign of smuggling, for vessels in distress. They carry a supply of Coston Flares to warn vessels venturing too near the coast or to notify ships in trouble that their signals have been received.

A cruising cutter—one of the largest of the Coast Guard floating units. These cutters are 328 feet long, have a great capacity for fuel and foodstuffs. If necessary, they can cruise for more than a month. Several such vessels are based at strategic points along the nation's coastline and, like all Coast Guard boats, would be of great value to the Navy in wartime.

A warship joins the fleet. A destroyer being launched at the Brooklyn Navy Yard. Each such destroyer commissioned represents an investment of between $3,400,000 and $3,750,000.

The President's flag is flown above the national emblem whenever the Commander-in-Chief visits a warship or reviews the fleet.

The Commander-in-Chief of the fleet and several members of his family aboard a battleship. In peacetime, of course, the President's naval duties are largely nominal, but at all times he works closely with the Chief of Naval Operations.

A warship in the making. The destroyer USS *Dale* up on the ways at the United States Navy Yard in Brooklyn in 1935, just before it was launched by author who was then Commandant of the Yard. It is about 342 feet long over all, weighs 1,395 tons, carries a complement of 162 officers and men, and is armed with five 5-inch guns in addition to torpedo tubes.

The USS *Idaho*, one of three battleships of the *New Mexico* class commissioned in 1917. Weighing 33,400 tons, it carries a complement of 1,323 officers and men, and has an overall length of 624 feet. It is armed with the following guns: twelve 14-inch, twelve 5-inch, eight 5-inch anti-aircraft, four salutes, twelve 50-caliber anti-aircraft.

shell was met by armor so thick that the shell could not penetrate—just as the effect of the underwater explosion of the torpedo was met by subdivision, and as the submarine was rendered less dangerous by the depth charge on board destroyers or other fast vessels.

The airplane is the latest weapon to undermine our confidence in the battleship. But we are finding that the airplane can be defeated. It is being done by anti-aircraft fire and by fighting types of airplanes with appropriate guns.

There have been and may yet be many other menaces to battleships, but we can feel sure that man's genius will find means to overcome them when the danger is known.

We have not, in consequence, lost faith in the power of our great surface warships to control the seas and make them safe for our merchant ships. But we must not neglect our other branches, particularly the airplane branch, because the battleship requires airplanes to ward off attacks of bombing planes just as it requires many destroyers to guard it from attacks by submarines.

Our naval air forces, like our warships, are not all of the same type. Each aircraft type has its primary function to perform and therefore each is different in some particular from another.

The Navy operates planes from aircraft carriers and from air bases. In carriers, the aircraft must all be land planes. The deck of a carrier is the landing field. Naval aircraft flown from bases ashore are both land planes and sea planes, and often amphibians.

The warships of the fleet such as battleships and cruisers also carry aircraft. These are sea planes and are fired from catapults, and after flight are hoisted back on board again with a derrick.

In our fleet today there will be found planes ranging all the way from the large patrol sea planes with crews of from six to a dozen men, to the small single-seater fighting plane. They are described in the appendix.

Progress in airplane design is advancing rapidly and will continue to advance, because we have in the last few years come to realize the vast importance of controlling the air over the sea. Navies are depending today upon their own air forces for their security, and to enable them to perform their function of commanding the sea.

Speed in all types of combat planes is being stepped up rapidly. The fighting plane is now up to 400 miles an hour and the bombing planes to nearly 300 miles an hour.

The Navy for the present has given up using airships, or lighter-than-air craft. In war they might prove useful, but they are very vulnerable targets for airplanes, and even in peace have proved unreliable in storms. A number of officers are sent yearly to the Air Station at Lakehurst, N. J., for training in handling of the several types of airships. These lighter-than-air ships are inflated with a gas lighter than air. Hydrogen is such a gas, but it is inflammable and dangerous. Therefore, the United States inflates its lighter-than-air ships with a noninflammable gas, helium, of which a considerable amount is available in the United States. Interest is still alive for lighter-than-air ships, and we may some day return to the use of these types.

The naval officer of the future must contend with many dangerous weapons that perhaps as yet have not been imagined. We can be confident that he will discover a means of defeating them, and the battle-tested types of warships, such as the battleship and the cruiser, will be important units of war fleets for many years to come.

CHAPTER XV

THE NAVY'S BIG JOB

UNDOUBTEDLY you already have a general idea of the duties of the fleet in which you hope to serve. But anyone headed for a naval career should know the Navy's duties in greater detail—its wider problems, the eventualities for which it is constantly preparing, and exactly what would happen if this country should be attacked.

While it is too much to assume that such an attack is inevitable, it must not be forgotten that such an attack might come. The Navy's job is to prepare for any possibility.

From the end of the war with Spain until within the last two decades, the authority of the Monroe Doctrine, defining "the principle of the limitation of European power and influence in the Western Hemisphere," was never challenged. It is being challenged now. The Navy is prepared to defend it.

In the most general terms, the Navy of the United States is for the purpose of defending:

(a) The continental territory from invasion by hostile armies carried across either ocean in troop transports, escorted by warships.

(b) The security of the territories and other possessions under our flag, lying outside our continental limits.

(c) The nation's rights to trade with all foreign countries on equal terms with other nations.

(d) Our mercantile marine on the high seas which carries the nation's import and export trade to all parts of the world.

Because of the nation's size, great wealth, and large population, the adequate defense of these important requisites make it necessary that we maintain a strong Navy; a Navy capable of exerting control of the seas in all areas that could be threatened by an aggressive sea power.

As we have said, the actual invasion of our country can hardly be successfully accomplished until after our fleet has been destroyed or bottled up in port by a superior enemy war fleet. Although important enough, the safety of our continent from invasion is the least of our Navy's worries.

Rather, it is the defense of possessions outside our continental limits, the maintenance of our nation's right to trade and obtain essential raw materials for our industries, and the assurance of free passage of our merchant ships across the seas to and from our ports. Although the invasion of these possessions or interference with these rights might not seem as serious a calamity as would be the invasion of the nation's shores, each of these possessions and rights must be amply safeguarded by the Navy.

The United States holds sovereignty over vast territory, and has vital interests in many parts of the world, yet our collective mind remains provincial. Many of our people cannot lift their imaginations above their own small communities, and today are raising their voices against adequate military and naval preparations, long neglected. Further neglect jeopardizes everything we hold dear. The fault lies in our inability in the past to accept our great world responsibilities.

The nation today requires a large naval and air force, and—with the world aflame—if it refuses to obtain them as quickly as possible, then instead of continuing as a great nation, it may find itself through the impact of hostile forces, shorn of the things that make a nation great.

Sea power defines the strength of a nation on the seas. If adequate, it gives the nation the freedom to use the seas for its own purposes, and prevents the curtailment of that freedom by the hostile action of other nations. Sea power is composed of three interdependent elements, all of which are equally important in the sum total of a nation's sea strength. These elements are: (1) warships and airplanes of all types; (2) naval and air bases; (3) merchant marine. If any one of these elements is inadequate, a nation's strength on the seas will suffer.

Naval strength consists of warships and airplanes. These are the fighting weapons. Naval and air bases lend support to naval strength in giving it mobility, or the power to operate at a distance. Merchant ships provide our naval strength the economic support required to exist in war.

Because of the existence of the British Navy the United States long has been neglecting its naval power in the Atlantic Ocean. Great Britain is considered by America as a friendly competitor on the seas, one that never would be an enemy.

The strength of Britain's naval power has always been

in her surface warships. Today naval weakness can exist
because of an insufficiency of air power to guard the
great surface warships. In consequence of weakness in air
power, the protection of vital lines of sea communication,
connecting together the many parts of an Empire, can
be menaced by an enemy with superior air power. Because of the destructive assaults of this new weapon,
the airplane, radical changes are being imposed upon
our former conceptions of strategy and tactics.

The great surface warships, such as the battleships,
cruisers, and so on, continuously must prove their un-
disputed ability to command the seas against all weapons
that man's ingenuity may invent.

When these leviathans of the seas are proved useless
for that great purpose by other weapons such as the
submarine and the airplane, then the old order on the
seas will collapse like a house of cards.

The best opinion among naval men seems to be that
both the submarines and the airplanes are vital forces
in any navy, but are only auxiliaries to naval strength.
They never can take the place of those dependable
weapons, the great surface warships, upon which the security at sea has always rested.

The United States, in the last decade or more, has
favored the Pacific, in which ocean its fleet has been
based. In that ocean the United States has a most extensive coast line. This coast line extends from the Mexican
border in a great arc, northward and westward, through
Alaska, its peninsula and islands, to within 700 miles
of the continent of Asia. That is a long coast line to
guard, and it can be accomplished best by an adequate
fleet and air force correctly based in that area. Such a

correctly located Naval base is at Pearl Harbor in the Hawaiian Islands.

The Hawaiian Islands lie geographically almost at the geometrical center of the arc of our coast line, at a distance of from 2,100 to 2,300 miles from all points on the arc, just within the area of operation of a fleet from Hawaii.

In addition to guarding this coast line, our fleet in the Pacific must also protect the Panama Canal, Guam and the Philippines, the latter islands being still under American sovereignty. And in addition to the concentrated fleet, the Navy maintains small forces of warships, such as cruisers, destroyers, submarines and air forces in the Orient, in Central American waters, and on special duty where foreign conditions can be observed and to protect American citizens abroad engaged in business.

The mission of our fleet in the Pacific is purely a defensive one. Defensive security of position in the Pacific is dependent upon something which is measured in terms of two factors: fleet strength and fleet mobility. These factors are complementary to each other. Fleet strength deals with power: types of warships and aircraft, numbers of surface, subsurface, and aircraft available for war use. Fleet mobility hinges upon facilities for repairs and upkeep of ships and planes, together with the provision of fuel and supplies; or in other words, naval bases.

The effective range of the fleet, which might be visioned as a projectile, is determined by the consideration that the fleet upon leaving a base may steam and operate for a certain definite space in time and distance, but must

The USS *West Virginia*, one of the three battleships commissioned in 1920 and 1921. As flagship of the fleet it carries a complement of 1,486 officers and men, otherwise it carries 1,407. With a maximum speed of about 21 knots, it is armed with the following guns: eight 16-inch, twelve 5-inch, eight 5-inch anti-aircraft, salutes, two machine guns, eleven anti-aircraft machine guns, and 21-inch torpedo tubes. The 16-inch guns can throw their projectiles well over 30,000 yards. It is protected, as all modern battleships, by minute internal subdivision of the hull.

Crew loading a gun in the casemate of a secondary battery on board a battleship.

The USS *Raleigh*, one of ten light cruisers of the Omaha class launched in the early 20's. Faster than heavy cruisers, these ships reached a speed of almost 35 knots in trials. They weigh about 7,050 tons, carry about 458 officers and men. Their principal weapons, the 6-inch guns, have a maximum range of 22,000 yards and are effective at 18,000 yards.

The USS *Erie*, a gunboat for patrol duty. About 330 feet long, it weighs 2,000 tons, and carries the following guns: four 5-inch, two 3-inch anti-aircraft. A seaplane is carried in the deck hangar. Its speed is 20 knots.

A crew loading and firing a broadside gun, their ears protected by cotton from the force of the charge.

The USS *Phoenix* is a light cruiser launched in 1936, one of the ships built to offset the Japanese ships of the "Mogami" class. They weigh about 10,000 tons and are more than 600 feet long. They are armed with fifteen 6-inch guns and eight 5-inch anti-aircraft. Cost: about $12,000,000 apiece.

The aircraft carrier USS *Lexington* lying off Niumalu Beach, Hawaii.

The United States river gun-boat *Mindanao*, similar to the *Panay* and also serving as a patrol ship in China. It weighs 560 tons, carries 78 officers and men, is 210 feet long, and armed with two 3-inch anti-aircraft guns, plus ten machine guns.

never lose the power of safe return to a base. A base is capable of renewing supplies of the fleet and restoring its strength. This effective range of a fleet will change with the size and consequent endurance of the many units of which it is composed. The distance is now accepted as 2,000 miles. Thus everything in the fleet in question, capable of inflicting damage—shot and shell, mines, torpedoes, fleets, and even armies in transports, operating from a naval base—may be regarded as missiles to be thrown from the base. The base itself, therefore, can be imagined as a great battery, arsenal, or storehouse of power, from which to project the fleet's fighting power. If we build a fleet without at the same time providing such a base for it, we shall commit the unforgivable error of providing a projectile without obtaining the gun to fire it.

The object of war on the seas has always been considered to be the control of communications. As a large area of the sea must be covered for this purpose, the navy ambitious to control must exercise such control with a large number of warships. Although the control of communications is most important to a sea-faring nation with a large merchant marine and owning a great world trade, a sea power such as Great Britain did not lose sight of the necessity to bring the enemy's fleet to action. Once that was successfully accomplished, the enemy's entire resistance on the seas could be destroyed.

Before the days of the submarine and the airplane, surface warships alone were used to control communications. The control of communications includes the destruction of the submarines and airplanes, for although these cannot control communications, they can destroy them. The present war is to be a test to prove whether the great surface warships with all their protecting forces can be prevented by the destroying weapon of the enemy from controlling communications, until finally there are no longer surface warships to exercise control.

The submarine and airplane, if superior in number, can take heavy toll of surface warships. The answer to this is many destroyers with depth charges against the submarines, and a large force of fighting planes against the enemy's bombing planes. An inferior surface navy will depend upon submarines and bombing planes to destroy the enemy's advantage. A nation greatly superior in air power can profit by that advantage if they are in close proximity to one another, as has been shown in recent wars. A vastly superior air power then may be capable of committing great havoc upon the enemy's warships and naval bases with bombs. In addition to destroying warships, bombing planes will endeavor to destroy the enemy's sea communications. It may thus be possible for a superior air power to defeat sea power in certain areas. Air power can destroy, but it is incapable of guarding communications by sea. Therefore surface warships will still be most important for a nation to own.

The great wars at sea have demonstrated the terrible destructiveness of the submarine and airplane. These are weapons comparatively new to the sea.

The United States, due to its geographical position, and its inherent policy of a strategical defensive, usually will await the attack of an enemy from overseas. Our frontiers extend from Maine to Puerto Rico, to Panama, to Puget Sound, to Alaska and its many islands, to Hawaii, to Guam, and to the Philippines. These frontiers can be guarded only by being strong enough to command the seas. The command of the sea can be won by the superior fleet, superior in morale and material.

From the broadest point of view, the defense of our sea frontiers involves the elements of defense in the following order: The fleet, including all offensive types of warships, the defense vessels and mine service; the fixed fortifications, and the mobile field armies.

In the conduct of naval war, accurate, timely information of enemy naval forces is an important consideration. An efficient secret service in both neutral and enemy territory should be organized in time of peace, and be in efficient operation upon the outbreak of war. This service will be capable of collecting information of enemy naval forces, transport and troops, which will guide our nation in its initial dispositions of fighting forces by sea, land and air.

Let us imagine our enemy fleet, possibly somewhat superior in numbers, yet hampered with a "train" of auxiliaries and troop ships, approaching our frontiers for the purpose of seizing an advance base from which to carry on war against us.

Our plan will call for offensive tactical operations against the enemy's fleet. Our Secret Service will, by radio or cable, inform the Government of the progress of enemy's mobilization. When the enemy fleet sails, word will be flashed across the sea. After the enemy has been swallowed up in the ocean waste no further word will be likely, unless it be a radio from a passing neutral ship that has, by chance, sighted the enemy's fleet without having its presence discovered. The enemy will screen his fleet by a cordon of fast scouts that will keep out of the screened area all vessels of whatever nationality.

As our defending fleet cannot afford to await blindly and meet the enemy on or near our coast, without information of his movements as long ahead of his arrival as possible, there then comes the need of "scouting." Information from our scouts permits our fleet to place itself in a position to intercept the enemy's fleet.

Beginning from the supposed vicinity of the enemy, our cruisers, acting as scouts, and even our submarines, will search for him. This is done by spacing vessels at intervals on a line, and the line of vessels moved across an area of ocean, in which the enemy's fleet is believed to be. After the enemy's fleet has been thus located, within a definite area, then the scouts will follow and track it as it advances.

This type of scouting, in the use of cruisers and long range submarines, is called "strategical" scouting. The scouting cruisers will have airplanes to cover wider areas. There may even be an aircraft carrier on this scouting duty.

"Tactical" scouting is performed in order to learn of the enemy's tactical formation, number and type of ships, and any other information, by the knowledge of which the disposition of the units of our fleet can be more scientifically arranged, in order to give battle in an advantageous tactical position. In "strategical" scouting, fighting is avoided, but in "tactical" scouting it must be accepted in order to penetrate screens and learn the strength of the enemy's fleet to be engaged in battle.

Our fleet, also screened by cruisers and destroyers against enemy torpedo attacks, especially enemy submarines, will, upon information received from its scouts, maneuver to place itself as near the probable path of the enemy fleet as possible.

As the two fleets approach, the scouting and screening may become more desperate. The enemy may send out scouts (cruisers) to locate our fleet in order to harass it by submarine, destroyer and air attack, and cause it to withdraw its scouting forces for defense purposes.

The actual battle will begin with a long-range duel and destroyer torpedo attacks and air attacks in waves from carriers. Destroyer attacks will be supported by cruisers. Air attacks will be guarded against by our fighting planes, flown from carriers to engage enemy bombers.

From the moment of deployment for battle, both fleets, without orders and frequently without signals, will carry out a prearranged tactical battle plan; the part each type will play having been carefully studied and rehearsed during peace in preparation for this battle.

Napoleon said, "Victory goes to him with the biggest battalions." Other things being equal, this is true; but on the sea, victory goes to him who has, through long years of patient study and practice, prepared himself to win.

Victory in battle will be decided in large part by the gunfire of the battleships. Other weapons will add to or detract from the final result. The torpedo and air bomb will take their heavy toll.

Let us draw here a word picture of the battleship, which will bear the brunt of the battle: All hands stand at their battle stations. The gun crews, bared to the waist, are in turrets and at casement guns. The anti-aircraft guns, located on the highest deck, will be pointed skyward ready to open fire upon airplanes attacking. The fire control parties will be at their stations, both high on the masts and in fire control stations far below decks, prepared to direct scientifically the fire of all the guns.

The Captain and Navigator will be in the armored conning tower, from which the warship is steered in action and its speed regulated. In the fire rooms are men to fire the oil burning boilers, and in the engine rooms men are present to regulate the flow of steam to the engines or turbines, according to directions from the conning tower, and by manipulation of valves, to pump out compartments that may become flooded because of shell penetration or torpedo explosions.

Besides these, there are the repair parties, to repair damages inflicted, the gunner's gang to give needed expert aid to guns that break down. In the magazines, far below decks, men will be loading the ammunition hoists to supply the guns far above. The doctors and their hospital corps men will be prepared to care for the wounded brought to them by the stretcher bearers.

Every water-tight door will be closed, and the thousand or more men below decks will perform their several duties, knowing little of what is going on above until a heavy list or a great explosion warns them that their ship is doomed. Even then, discipline, drilled into them in peace, will have taught them how to evacuate their dangerous positions, and reach safety without panic.

We sincerely hope, of course, that our battleships will not be called into such a battle. But the Navy must prepare for the eventuality. That is why the government is looking now toward an enlarged personnel and an expanded fleet.

Our fleet in the Pacific, based on Hawaii, is adequate for its defensive mission, with the exception of defending Guam and the Philippines. The security of these possessions demands a far larger fleet than the one now available.

In this unsettled world of today, America cannot feel secure until it knows that the youth of our country is trained in the art of modern war and can handle with expertness all the modern weapons needed to defend our soil from invasion. In addition, the nation will wish to be assured that the Navy and its air force is adequately numerous and competent to protect the sovereignty under our flag, and the moral obligations of our Monroe Doctrine.

The Panama Canal, giving passage from one ocean to the other, is America's life line. The Canal itself is strongly defended by the Army. In the Atlantic are outlying island positions: Puerto Rico, St. Thomas, and Guantanamo, Cuba, some of which are being heavily fortified and prepared to be used as outposts to support the Canal defenses. An enemy from overseas intent upon attacking the Canal, would first attempt to occupy these defensive positions.

America's fleet at its present strength, based in the Pacific, can defend Alaska, the coast line of the continent, and the Panama Canal from attacks coming from the westward. But that leaves the Atlantic without a defending fleet. This is the reason for the present aim to build warships and planes in order that the Navy would be able to defend America in both oceans. Then with the Panama Canal open, the entire fleet could be concentrated wherever danger threatened.

America's greatest concern is from attacks by air. The natural defense is to build a huge air force and sufficient air bases at strategical locations to defend the nation's most vulnerable possessions. At the same time the nation should make certain that no enemy obtains a foothold to be used in operating its air forces against our country. From the standpoint of hemisphere security alone, the United States must not permit the seizure of islands that can be used as bases for warships or airplanes in attacks upon any part of the American continents. Such positions are Iceland, Greenland, the Azores, the islands of the West Indies, and the territory of any one of the twenty Latin republics. When America has provided itself for fighting on the seas with weapons so powerful in the aggregate that even the strongest sea power will hesitate to attack, and when it adds to these purely naval weapons an air power that will guard us from surprise attacks in both oceans, then—behind this formidable defense—the country can with assured safety develop its industrial strength and take its place as a stabilizing factor in this confused world.

CHAPTER XVI

THE ULTIMATE GOAL

HERE I have tried to show you something of a naval officer's life, what qualities he needs, how his natural abilities are forged, his mind and his body equipped at the Naval Academy and in the fleet. I have tried to show how he steps from rank to rank, the glorious traditions he has inherited, the exciting and honorable career that faces him as an officer in a tremendous, far-flung military organization standing guard over a great country.

Here my job ends and yours begins. If your heart is full of the Navy, none of the rigors that have been stressed (rather than have you believe Navy-life is one round of fun) will change your mind. The difficulties are all part of the picture. They are the Naval officer's bulwark and his strength—from accomplishment to accomplishment he goes on and on, learning and living, accepted more and more responsibility, growing under it. He bends his back to the task, but because he does he has more fun when he plays.

You have found perhaps that most professional men in civilian life have soured on their jobs. You ask a newspaperman how to be a newspaperman and he tells you to be anything else, but never *that*. You ask a banker how to be a banker and he tells you to be anything else, but never *that*. And so it goes. But not in the Navy. The life carries no better recommendation than the fact that every naval officer I have ever known—and I've known a lot of them—would rather swim to China than change his job with anyone. Of course he always wants to go up and onward inside that Navy. That is the vital, competitive spirit that keeps the Navy vigorous.

In the last analysis, however, nothing I can say—or anything anyone can say—can set your goal for you. We can only tell you what it is like to be a naval officer. The final decision to go after a commission with all your energy rests with you. I happen to think it is worth the work it takes. And if you do, too, the chances are that you'll get it.

And so, "lights out," and good luck!

APPENDIX A

DETAILED DESCRIPTION OF COURSES OF STUDY AT THE NAVAL ACADEMY (OUTLINED BRIEFLY IN CHAPTER VII).

SEAMANSHIP AND NAVIGATION. Practical instruction in seamanship begins with the midshipman's entrance into the Academy and continues throughout the four-year course. It includes practice cruises during the second and fourth years, a one month's coastal cruise and elementary instruction in aviation during the third and fourth years. The practical instruction includes progressive drills in handling all types of boats, knotting, splicing, compass, log and lead, ground tackle, elementary signals, communications and flight.

The study of navigation begins during the first two years with preliminary practical instruction in the use of charts and instruments given during drill periods. Intensive instruction in chart work and piloting is given during the summer of the third year in conjunction with the practice of piloting during the second class coastal cruise. The third summer also includes an elementary course, including practical work in marine surveying. Instruction in geonavigation extends throughout the third academic year, the practice cruise, and the fourth academic year, when a progressive study is made covering the compass, sailings, further work in piloting, a short course in nautical astronomy, various types of solutions of sights, rising and setting of sun and moon, use of azimuth, tide and current tables, mooring board, and aerial navigation. Three periods each month are devoted to practical work. Other periods are used for practical instruction as found desirable.

During the first class cruise the midshipmen perform navigational duty on board ship. They are required to take sights, work them out, and to locate the ship's position by these sights and dead reckoning. Piloting is taught under circumstances which enable the midshipmen to see how the ship is handled. The midshipmen assist in compensating the compass. The value and use of the gyrocompass are demonstrated.

ORDNANCE AND GUNNERY. During the summer of fourth-class year practical instruction in service rifles and pistols is given, including firing of the service rifle, and pistol marksman, sharpshooter, and expert courses. Preliminary practical instruction is also given with the ordnance equipment in Dahlgren Hall. During the academic year the fourth class is given rifle instruction on the rifle range and gun-loading drills. The course during the third-class year consists of pistol shooting on the range, instruction in machine guns, landing guns, and gun loading. In the summer of the second-class year, midshipmen complete the Pensacola Ground School aviation machine-gun course; this course includes aviation machine-gun firing, clay-pigeon firing, chemical warfare lectures, and practical instruction with gas warfare equipment and materials. Each midshipman is required to undergo training with gas mask and protective clothing in a gas chamber. In addition, midshipmen are given instruction in firing other small weapons, such as the landing gun, the service automatic rifle, the Thompson submachine gun, the 50-caliber antiaircraft machine gun. The course for the second class during the academic year includes guns and their mechanisms, rangefinders, torpedoes and the control of torpedo fire, mines, and the fire control of secondary and main batteries. First-class year is devoted primarily to fire control of all types of batteries, but especially of the main battery.

The practical work at the Naval Academy is supplemented during the third class and first class by summer cruises on battleships, and by the second-class cruise of one month on destroyers. During these cruises, lectures, practical instruction, and drills are designed to prepare midshipmen thoroughly for the future duties on board ship. During the destroyer cruise a visit is made to the Naval Proving Ground, Dahlgren, Virginia, where a special program of test and experimental firing is conducted for their benefit; a visit is also made to the Naval Gun Factory, Washington, D. C., and to the Naval Torpedo Station, Newport, R. I. At the torpedo station midshipmen observe the firing of the torpedoes from the testing barge. Short-range target practice, using turret, broadside, and antiaircraft guns, is carried on during the last part of the battleship cruises. An illumination exercise at night using star-shells is also conducted. The first class perform the duties of officers during these gunnery exercises.

The study of naval ordnance begins with theoretical instruction during the first academic term, second-class year. The subject includes service explosives, interior ballistics, gun construction, guns, gun mounts, armor, and projectiles. In the second term the course embraces torpedoes and mines, the fundamental applications of the theories of exterior ballistics to solution of the trajectory, the construction of range tables, and safety precautions. In the first-class year, exterior ballistics, fire-control methods and equipment, fleet-gunnery methods and instructions, and the duties of officers in the gunnery department aboard ship are studied.

Textbooks and service publications are used which have been specially written by experienced officers of the United States Navy for instruction of the midshipmen and junior officers. Besides the study of these, a series of lectures on practical ordnance and gunnery is given by officers from the Navy Department or the fleet.

MARINE ENGINEERING. Courses are as follows—

Fourth Class (First Year)—Summer and First Terms, beginning with fourth-class year: *Descriptive geometry and mechanical drawing.*

Fourth Class (First Year)—Second Term: *Engineering drawing.*

Third Class (Second Year)—First Term: *Engineering materials; Naval reciprocating engines; Naval auxiliary machinery; Boilers.*

Third Class (Second Year)—Second Term: *Turbines; Mechanisms.*

Second Class (Third Year)—First Term: *Thermodynamics.*

Second Class (Third Year)—Second Term: *Heat transfer and thermodynamics as applied to naval machinery.*

First Class (Fourth Year)—First Term: *Internal-combustion engines; Metallurgy.*

First Class (Fourth Year)—Second Term: *Metallurgy.*

The midshipmen receive practical work as follows—

Fourth Class (First Year)—Summer: *Pattern shop; Machine shop; Coppersmith shop, forge shop, foundry; Elementary engineering; Engineering materials.*

Fourth Class (First Year)—Winter Practical Exercises: *Precision measurements; Boilers and engines.*

Third Class (Second Year)—Summer Practice Cruise: *Tour of inspection of engine and boiler compartments and auxiliary stations; study and sketching (where applicable).*

Third Class (Second Year)—Winter Practical Exercises: *Shops; Model room; Mechanisms laboratory.*

Second Class (Third Year)—Summer Term at Naval Academy: *Steam laboratory; Engineering calculations; Metals laboratory; Internal-combustion-engine laboratory; Instrument laboratory; Submarine instruction; Destroyer cruise.*

Second Class (Third Year)—Winter Laboratory Exercises: *Liquid and gas measuring devices in machinery used in the Navy; testing performance of auxiliary machinery.*

First Class (Fourth Year)—Summer Practice Cruise: *Administration of the engineering department of a warship.*

First Class (Fourth Year)—Winter Laboratory Exercises: *Metals laboratory; Internal-combustion-engine laboratory; Instrument laboratory; Damage control laboratory.*

MATHEMATICS. Fourth Class (First Year)—First Term: *Solid mensuration; Algebra; Plane trigonometry; Spherical trigonometry.*

Fourth Class (First Year)—Second Term: *Plane and Solid analytical geometry.*

Third Class (Second Year)—First Term: *Calculus.*

Third Class (Second Year)—Second Term: *Integration; Mechanics.*

Second Class (Third Year)—First Term: *Mechanics.*

ELECTRICAL ENGINEERING. The course of instruction given

by this department includes chemistry, physics, direct-current electricity, alternating-current electricity, and radio.

Fourth Class (First Year)—First and Second Terms: The year is devoted to the study of general inorganic chemistry with laboratory work. In addition, lectures and demonstration lectures are given on the practical application of chemistry to the naval service.

Third Class (Second Year)—First and Second Terms: The subject of physics is taken up during the whole of the third-class year and includes the study of mechanics, heat, sound, and light, with the application of the various laws and principles in these branches of the subject.

Second Class (Third Year)—Second Term: During the three months' summer term at the Naval Academy the second class is given three separate courses: (a) Lecture course in the application of physics, including the flight of projectiles, gyroscopes, listening devices, theory of flight, and optical instruments; (b) Electrical laboratory course; (c) Radio operators' course.

Second Class (Third Year)—First and Second Terms: The entire year is devoted to the study of magnetism, electrostatics, direct-current circuits, and electrical machinery. Laboratory work parallels the text and covers the following: magnetic fields, induced electromotive force; measurements of electrical quantities, etc. A series of lectures is given throughout both terms. These lectures also cover the practice in the electrical department aboard vessels of the fleet.

First Class (Fourth Year)—Practice Cruise: While on the practice cruise one-third of the time assigned to engineering is devoted to electrical instruction. This includes watchstanding and lectures as well as notebook work.

First Class (Fourth Year)—First and Second Terms: The first class continues the subject of alternating-current electricity, including electronics and radio. The second term is devoted to basic principles of thermionics and applications to general electricity as well as to radio.

ENGLISH, HISTORY, AND GOVERNMENT. Courses in English, history, and government are taught for the most part by the same instructors, and the aim is to correlate the instruction so that the different fields shall, when possible, contribute one to another.

Fourth Class (First Year)—Summer Term: Midshipmen of the entering class are introduced to the Naval Academy Library, and for eleven weeks have a weekly reading period in the library or museum. By lectures and other means they are guided in their readings, their attention is directed to the importance of naval traditions and to the significance of the great names in the Service, some of which they are meeting for the first time.

Fourth Class (First Year)—First and Second Terms: *Composition and Literature.* Emphasis is placed on organization and the principles which underline effective composition. The theme is considered as a whole, and as the paragraphs, sentences, and words constituting it. Effort is made to form correct habits of writing and speaking and to gain ease of expression to the end that the chief attention may be given to the thought rather than to the medium of communication. Practice is held in public speaking, a form of composition every naval officer is certain to have occasion to use.

Third Class (Second Year): *Naval History, Government.*

Second Class (Third Year)—Summer Term: A course of lectures on Trends of Social and Economic Events. *General Reading; Modern Thought; American Foreign Policy.*

First Class (Fourth Year): *Modern European History; Technical Composition; After-Dinner Speaking.*

LANGUAGES. Department of Languages conducts courses in French, Spanish, German, and Italian, with particular emphasis on naval phases of interpreting. Each entering class is divided into groups approximately as follows: French and Spanish, 40 per cent each; German and Italian, 10 per cent each. Upon completion of the language course, midshipmen are offered the opportunity of qualifying as interpreters in the language studied. Those who successfully pass the examination are certified to the Navy Department for the appropriate entry in their official records.

HYGIENE. The courses include: Physical education; Personal hygiene; Physical training, the benefits of muscular activity: Preventable diseases; vision; simple rules for maintaining health: Oral prophylaxis and care of the teeth.

The first class is given a course during the second term in general physiology and bacteriology; naval hygiene and first aid; and the effects of narcotics and alcohol, using a textbook compiled especially for midshipmen. The course includes: Elementary physiology; Elementary bacteriology; Physiology of the nervous system; Venereal diseases; Community hygiene; Ship hygiene; Hygiene of submarine diving; Camp hygiene; Aviation medicine; Medical aspects of chemical warfare; Practical first aid.

PHYSICAL TRAINING. In this department midshipmen are trained in the principles of health and recreation. In addition, they are given instruction in the various branches of physical drill and athletics in order to qualify them as leaders and coaches of the athletics in the fleet.

Athletic training is progressive. In the first year, as fourth classmen, all midshipmen on entering the Academy are given an initial examination in which they are tested in strength, posture, gymnasium ability and swimming capability. Photographic and graphic records are made at this time.

Each year certain requirements are insisted upon. For instance, in swimming the midshipmen in the first year must swim for 5 minutes—demonstrating the crawl, back, right and left side strokes. There also are standard requirements in gymnasium work, boxing, wrestling, and dancing.

The second year midshipmen must swim 120 yards in 3 minutes, using each of the important strokes. The strength requirement is increased, as are also gymnasium requirements. Correct posture is emphasized and insisted upon.

The third year, swimming ability must be increased to 160 yards in 4 minutes, using the standard strokes. Life-saving and knowledge of resuscitation are taught; also diving in correct form. Strength, gymnasium work, and posture are again emphasized.

In the fourth year, instruction covers a wider field: Midshipmen are taught self-defense, rough and tumble, boxing, wrestling, and golf.

Athletics are voluntary, but facilities are provided throughout the four years for all kinds of athletics, and midshipmen are strongly encouraged to take part in athletic contests. The "N" insignia for athletes is awarded for excellence in the recognized sports and is highly prized.

APPENDIX B

DUTIES OF THE CHIEF OF NAVAL OPERATIONS, APPOINTED BY THE PRESIDENT

Supervision of:
1. Office of Naval Intelligence.
2. The Division of Fleet Training.
3. Operation of the Communication Service.
4. Naval Districts.
5. Vessels assigned to the Naval Reserve.
6. The Marine Corps.
7. Operation of Coast Guard vessels serving in the Navy.
8. Planning for war, and all strategic and tactical matters.
9. Organization and training of the fleet for war.
10. Maneuvers of the fleet.
11. Gunnery exercises of naval ships.
12. Inspection Division.

THE BUREAU OF NAVIGATION

This bureau keeps the records of every officer and enlisted man, active, retired or in the reserve. It orders the transfer of personnel from one duty to another.

Under the bureau are a number of activities, among them being:

1. The recruiting service and training stations to which enlisted recruits are sent for preliminary training.

2. Naval discipline and training in general of both active and reserve personnel.

3. Naval Home, where retired officers and men are taken if necessary.

4. Naval Observatory, where observations are taken to establish accurate time and broadcast the time signals.

5. Hydrographic offices, where hydrographic and navigational information is collected, and through the medium of charts and publications is given to the world.

6. Naval Academy.

7. Naval War College at Newport, R. I., where officers are taught the art of naval war.

8. Post-Graduate School at Annapolis.

THE BUREAU OF ORDNANCE

The function of this bureau is to arm the Navy. It is charged with design and procurement of arms and ammunition, armor, torpedoes, mines, and depth charges.

It maintains the following naval stations:

Location and Function of U. S. Naval Stations

1. Gun factory at Washington, D. C., where guns, gun mounts, cartridge cases, turret machinery, etc., are made. About 8,000 civilians are employed.

2. Powder factory, Indianhead, Md. Here part of the smokeless powder for the Navy is manufactured. About 600 civilians are employed.

3. Proving grounds, Dahlgren, Va. Here ordnance is proved, and experimental ordnance work done. About 300 civilians are employed.

4. Torpedo station, Newport, R. I. At this place torpedoes and torpedo parts are made, torpedoes tested, modernized, and converted. About 4,000 civilians are employed.

5. Torpedo station, Keyport, Wash. Similar but less extensive services than the station at Newport, R. I. About 100 civilians are employed.

6. Mine depot, Yorktown, Va. This station is charged with the storage and overhaul of mines, filling of aircraft bombs, etc. About 200 civilians are employed.

7. Ordnance plant, Baldwin, Long Island, N. Y. Here the loading of illuminating projectiles and flares is done. About 200 civilians are employed.

8. Ordnance plant, South Charleston, W. Va. Here an

armor and projectile plant was built during the World War. At present inactive.

Location of Ammunition Depots Maintained by Bureau of Ordnance

Hingham, Mass.; Iona Island, N. Y.; Fort Lafayette, N. Y.; Lake Denmark, N. J.; Fort Mifflin, Pa.; St. Juliens Creek, Va.; Hawthorne, Nev.; Mare Island, Cal.; Puget Sound, Wash.; Oahu Island, T. H.; and Cavite, P. I. In these ammunition depots a total of about 15,000 civilians are employed.

THE BUREAU OF AERONAUTICS

The purpose of this bureau is to equip the Navy with airplanes of maximum performance, reliability, and endurance. It has cognizance of the design, construction, testing, and repair of aircraft for the Navy and Marine Corps. This bureau is vastly interested in the training of naval aviators, and has considerable authority in their procurement and instruction, both in the active personnel and the reserve.

The Navy maintains airplane establishments as follows:

1. Air Station, Lakehurst, N. J. At this station lighter-than-air training is done and a parachute school is maintained.

2. Aircraft factory, Philadelphia, Pa. At this factory the following activities are accomplished: airplanes and engines manufactured, airplanes overhauled, the purchase and distribution of spare parts and maintenance material for airplanes, experimental work in airplane design and construction. About 1,000 civilians are employed.

3. Air Station, Anacostia, D. C. This is a utility and transportation station; also an important airplane testing station, a landing place for both sea planes and land planes. About 400 civilians are employed.

4. Air Station, Norfolk, Va. This is the main east coast base for fleet aircraft. Its duties include overhaul of planes and special phases of testing new airplanes. It is a landing

place for both sea planes and land planes. Employs about 400 civilians.

5. Air Station, Pensacola, Fla. At this station heavier-than-air training is accomplished for the Navy. Graduates about 500 a year. Overhauls aircraft. It is a landing place for both sea planes and land planes. Employs about 700 civilians.

6. Air Station, Seattle, Wash. This is a minor base for fleet air squadrons. Used also for reserve aviation activities.

7. Air Station, San Diego, Cal. This is the main west coast base for fleet air craft. Major distribution point for airplane spare parts and maintenance material. It furnishes landing and overhaul facilities for both sea planes and land planes. Employs about 300 civilians.

8. Fleet Air Base, Pearl Harbor, T. H. This is the base for Pacific patrol squadrons. Provides facilities for basing, operating, and training of air squadrons. Provides a landing place for sea planes and land planes. Few civilians are employed. Overhaul and maintenance work done mostly by Navy personnel.

9. Fleet Air Base, Coco Solo, C. Z. Furnishes base for fleet aircraft and primary base for Navy patrol squadrons. Provides facilities for basing, operating, and training of air squadrons. Provides a landing place for sea planes and land planes. Work done mostly by Navy personnel.

There are small naval stations at Guam; Samoa; Guantanamo, Cuba; and San Juan, Puerto Rico, where minor repair work can be accomplished upon warships that might visit these stations.

THE BUREAU OF CONSTRUCTION AND REPAIR

The functions of this bureau are:

1. Design of naval ships which of necessity embody features desired by other bureaus and therefore require close co-ordination of this bureau with all of the Navy Department.

2. Operation of the experimental model basin in which types of hull design are tested.

3. Supply of such material as diving gear, gas masks, and mine-sweeping equipment.

BUREAU OF YARDS AND DOCKS

The functions of this bureau are:

1. Design and construction of the Navy's public works, including buildings, drydocks, marine railways, wharves, power plants, and bridges.

2. Heating, lighting, and telephone systems in naval property ashore, such as Navy Yards and Naval Bases.

3. Designs of locomotives, derricks, trucks, all vehicles, even horses and teams, and their operation at naval stations.

THE BUREAU OF ENGINEERING

The function of this bureau is the design and procurement of all engineering plants and auxiliary engineering equipment for the Navy. It is now consolidated with the Bureau of Construction and Repair.

The Bureau maintains shore establishments as follows:

1. Naval Research Laboratory, Anacostia, D. C. At this place fundamental research is conducted upon such subjects of naval interest as radio, sound, physical metallurgy, thermodynamics, chemistry, mechanics, physical optics, etc.

2. Engineering Experiment Station, Annapolis, Md. Here is accomplished testing and investigation of auxiliary machinery, petroleum products, Diesel engines and metals.

3. Naval Boiler Laboratory, Philadelphia, Pa. Here are tested new boilers, boiler fittings, etc.

4. Materials Test Laboratory, New York, N. Y. Here tests of materials and instruments for electrical installations are made. The laboratory is under the joint cognizance of the Bureau of Engineering and Bureau of Construction and Repair, recently consolidated by Executive order.

Small naval stations are located at the following points: Guam; Samoa; Guantanamo, Cuba, and San Juan, Puerto Rico. All of these are equipped to make minor repairs upon warships that might visit them.

BUREAU OF SUPPLIES AND ACCOUNTS

The functions of this bureau are:

1. Supplying and accounting for the materials and funds used by the Navy.

2. Administers the procuring, purchase, receipt, custody, warehousing and issue of supplies, fuel, and other material.

3. Administers the "Naval Supply Account Fund," from which are purchased stores and materials for general use.

4. Upkeep and operation of the Naval Clothing Depot, the coffee-roasting plants, etc.

5. Administrative supervision over fuel plants, commissary activities, supply depots and warehouses at navy yards and stations.

6. Estimates funds for freight, fuel, clothing, pay, allowances, subsistence and transportation of Navy personnel.

7. In cooperation with design bureaus, recommends location, type, size, and interior arrangements of storehouses ashore, and the equipment and arrangement of supply activity's spaces afloat.

8. Disbursement of funds for the payment of naval and civil pay rolls, and for articles and services procured for the Navy, as well as keeping all money and property accounts.

BUREAU OF MEDICINE AND SURGERY

The functions of this bureau are:

1. Medical care for the Navy and Marine Corps and certain insular civil communities administered by the Navy.

2. Maintains 18 general hospitals, dispensaries, and medical supply depots on shore.

3. Administers medical facilities and services on board every naval vessel in active commission, including hospital ships of the Navy.

The Medical Department includes approximately 900 commissioned medical officers, 250 dental officers, 390 nurses, 4,000 hospital corpsmen, and 1,200 civilian employees.

OFFICE OF THE JUDGE ADVOCATE GENERAL

This office is the legal department of the Navy, and has cognizance of all matters of law which involve the Navy.

It renders opinions on the legality of proceedings in civil courts relating to insurance contracts and patents, and upon legal features of naval courts-martial, courts of inquiry, boards of investigation and inquests.

Bills and resolutions introduced into the Congress are examined by this office. Proposed legislation arising in the Navy Department to be submitted to Congress are drafted by the office.

NAVAL EXAMINING AND RETIRING BOARDS

The Naval Examining Board is directly under the Secretary of the Navy. This board of naval officers conducts the examinations which every officer must take as he advances through the successive ranks from Ensign to Admiral.

The Naval Retiring Board, composed of commissioned line officers and medical officers, examines and reports upon the mental and physical fitness of officers ordered before it, to determine their qualifications to perform active service.

In addition to the above bureaus of the Navy Department concerned in the administration of the Navy, there are several other boards, agencies and committees, such as:

NAVAL PETROLEUM AND OIL SHALE RESERVES

Under this office is administered Naval Petroleum Reserves, on land where oil is known to exist and which has been set aside for the exclusive use of the Navy. There are four of these reserves in the country, and the estimated number of barrels of oil in them are in the hundreds of millions.

JOINT BOARD

Composed of both Army and Navy officers, this board studies and reports on matters requiring cooperation between the Army and Navy.

AERONAUTICAL BOARD

This board, composed of officers of both services, studies, investigates and reports upon questions affecting jointly the development and employment of aviation of both services. The purpose is to prevent duplication of efforts and to secure cooperation and coordination between Army Air Corps and Naval Aviation.

ARMY AND NAVY MUNITIONS BOARD

This board is for the purpose of coordinating the planning for acquiring munitions and supplies required by the War and Navy Departments for war purposes, or to meet the needs of any joint war plan.

JOINT MERCHANT VESSEL BOARD

This board inspects and classifies merchant vessels for possible use in war, either as naval auxiliary vessels or troop transports.

LOCAL JOINT PLANNING COMMITTEES

In all Army Corps Areas and Naval Districts, joint committees are appointed to coordinate the activities of both services in such local areas.

APPENDIX C

TYPES OF NAVAL AIRPLANES USED BY THE UNITED STATES NAVY

FIGHTING (VE)

Single-seater, small, fast, highly maneuverable, flown by one pilot. Operates from aircraft carrier, but can be flown from air field ashore. Their mission is to attack enemy aircraft using machine guns. Can be armed with light bombs and used as dive bomber against surface warships and submarines on the top of the sea.

BOMBING (VB)

These vary in size, depending upon the size of bombs carried. Two general classes of bombing operations are in use: horizontal and dive bombing.

TORPEDO (VT)

These carry torpedoes similar to those used by surface warships. Torpedo planes can also carry bombs for horizontal bombing. These big planes must depend upon surprise, speed, and smoke screens to get within striking distance of an enemy ship. The torpedo must be dropped from an altitude close to the water, else the impact of the weapon in striking the sea will derange the intricate mechanism to make the torpedo run straight for its goal.

OBSERVATION (VO)

The large naval guns today can fire at ranges where the target actually is beneath the horizon. It is necessary in controlling the fire of these guns to know where, relative to the target, the shells of salvos are falling. Even from the highest position in the firing ship, the hull of the target ship cannot be seen at ranges of upwards of 30,000 yards, at which distance naval battles may be fought. Other means of observing the fall of salvos must be employed. These observation planes fly high over the target, observe the fall of shells, and radio back information for the change of elevation and for lateral displacement, to cause the next salvo to hit the target. These observation planes are carried on board all battleships and cruisers to be used for this purpose.

SCOUT (VS)

These planes are used for scouting out enemy positions. They are called the "eyes" of the fleet. By their alertness and intelligent employment advance information is obtained by a Commander in Chief of a fleet regarding the enemy's whereabouts. This information is transmitted by radio and thus enables the Admiral to know his enemy's strength and the disposition of his warships. The characteristics of the scout planes are highest possible speed, long cruising radius, and reliable radio equipment. They usually are two-seater planes and are carried in both aircraft carriers and cruisers.

PATROL (VP)

These are great flying boats capable of flying across wide expanses of ocean. They carry the latest radio equipment and the fullest supply of necessary navigational instruments. They operate either from land bases or from aircraft tenders built for the purpose. They are used in the patrol of both coastal zones and for coastal scouting. They are used also as long-range scouts for the fleet.

In addition to those combatant types of planes mentioned above, the Navy maintains several other types, such as the Training Plane (VN), the General Utility Plane (VJ), Transport (VR), and Experimental Planes (VX).

CPSIA information can be obtained at www.ICGtesting.com
Printed in the USA
BVOW02s0958210314

348378BV00011B/299/P